40-Day Journey with Parker J. Palmer

Other books in the

40-DAY

Journey

Series

40-Day Journey with Joan Chittister
Beverly Lanzetta, Editor

40-Day Journey with Dietrich Bonhoeffer
Ron Klug, Editor

40-Day Journey with Martin Luther
Gracia M. Grindal, Editor

40-Day Journey with Kathleen Norris
Kathryn Haueisen, Editor

40-Day Journey with Julian of Norwich
Lisa Dahill, Editor

40-DAY

Journey

WITH PARKER J. PALMER

40-Day Journey Series

Henry F. French, Editor

Augsburg Books

Minneapolis

Cover design by Laurie Ingram; Cover photo © Sharon Palmer. Used by permission.
Book design: PerfecType, Nashville, Tenn.

Library of Congress Cataloging-in-Publication Data
Henry F. French, editor.
40-day journey with Parker J. Palmer / Henry F. French, editor.
    p. cm. — (40-day journey series)
Includes bibliographical references.
ISBN 978-0-8066-8046-0 (alk. paper)
1. Spiritual life—Christianity. 2. Devotional exercises. 3. Palmer,
Parker J. I. French, Henry F. II. Title: Forty day journey with Parker J.
Palmer.
BV4501.3.A15 2008
242—dc22
        2008017882

Manufactured in Canada.

CONTENTS

SERIES INTRODUCTION

Imagine spending forty days with a great spiritual guide who has both the wisdom and the experience to help you along the path of your own spiritual journey. Imagine being able to listen to and question spiritual guides from the past and the present. Imagine being, as it were, mentored by women and men who have made their own spiritual journey and have recorded the landmarks, detours, bumps in the road, potholes, and wayside rests that they encountered along the way—all to help others (like you) who must make their own journey.

The various volumes in Augsburg Books's *40-Day Journey Series* are all designed to do just that—to lead you where your mind and heart and spirit long to go. As Augustine once wrote: *"You have made us for yourself, O Lord, and our heart is restless until it rests in you."* The wisdom you will find in the pages of this series of books will give you the spiritual tools and direction to find that rest. But there is nothing quietistic in the spirituality you will find here. Those who would guide you on this journey have learned that the heart that rests in God is one that lives with deeper awareness, deeper creativity, deeper energy, and deeper passion and commitment to the things that matter to God.

An ancient Chinese proverb states the obvious: the journey of a thousand miles begins with the first step. In a deep sense, books in the *40-Day Journey Series* are first steps on a journey that will not end when the forty days are over. No one can take the first step (or any step) for you.

Imagine that you are on the banks of the Colorado River. You are here to go white-water rafting for the first time and your guide has just described the experience, telling you with graphic detail what to expect. It sounds both exciting and frightening. You long for the experience but are somewhat disturbed, anxious, uncertain in the face of the danger that promises to accompany you on the journey down the river. The guide gets into the raft. She will accompany you on the journey, *but she can't take the journey for you.* If you want to experience the wildness of the river, the raw beauty of the canyon, the camaraderie of adventurers, and the mystery of a certain oneness with nature (and nature's creator), then you've got to get in the raft.

This book in your hand is like that. It describes the journey, provides a "raft," and invites you to get in. Along with readings from your spiritual guide, you will find scripture to mediate on, questions to ponder, suggestions for personal journaling, guidance in prayer, and a prayer for the day. If done faithfully each day, you will find the wisdom and encouragement you need to integrate meaningful spiritual insights and practices into your daily life. And when the 40-day journey is over, it no longer will be the guide's description of the journey that stirs your longing for God but *your own experience* of the journey that grounds your faith and life and keeps you on the path.

I would encourage you to pick up other books in the series. There is only one destination, but many ways to get there. Not everything in every book will work for you (we are all unique), but in every book you will find much to help you discover your own path on the journey to the One in whom we all "live and move and have our being" (Acts 17:28).

May all be well with you on the journey.
Henry F. French, Series Editor

PREFACE

The title of Parker J. Palmer's first book—*The Promise of Paradox: A Celebration of the Contradictions in the Christian Life* (1980)—is a window on his thought, attitudes, values, and approach to the apparent incongruities of life. It is also a window on what you can expect to encounter in *40-Day Journey with Parker J. Palmer*.

In his introduction to *The Promise of Paradox*, the late Henri J. M. Nouwen, well-known and highly regarded spiritual writer and close friend and mentor of Parker J. Palmer, noted that the book was:

> the beautiful fruit of contradictions which became paradoxes: the
> contradiction between an educational success story and the growing
> need for simple community life; the contradiction between acceptance
> in respectable circles and the feeling of alienation and separation;
> the contradiction between speaking and lecturing about community
> and the loneliness of a highly individualized suburban existence; the
> contradiction between speaking more and more about religion and
> knowing God less and less. Parker lived these contradictions. . . .
> Living these contradictions brought him to insights, ideas and per-
> spectives which could have been found in no other way.[1]

As Palmer discovered, contradictions that are embraced and lived in are more often than not transformed into paradoxes that lead one into the deep realities of the soul where our own truth can be found, embraced, and lived. In the pages that lie ahead, you will be encouraged to grapple with the outer contradictions of our society and culture as well as with the inner contradictions of your own life. In the process, you may well discover these contradictions transform into paradoxes and, if you are able to embrace the paradoxes, you will be drawn toward the experience of *A Hidden Wholeness*[2] and the truths of your soul.

There are many apparent contradictions that we often fail to examine and fail to resolve, resulting in an often conflicted and confused life. On your 40-day journey, daily readings from Palmer's many books, along with wisdom from the Bible, questions to ponder, and suggestions for journaling, will invite you to examine many seeming contradictions with the goal of learning what they have to teach:

- the inner life—the outer life
- the divided life—the undivided life
- inner darkness—inner light
- the darkness of the world—the light of the world
- scarcity—abundance
- solitude—community
- action—contemplation
- weakness—strength
- liability—giftedness
- living while dying—dying while living

As you grapple with these contradictions you will find yourself thinking about reality in new ways. A major theme of Palmer's life and work is a concern with being real, with becoming aware of (and stripping away) the illusions that blind us to reality and the truth about ourselves. Indeed, to spend time with Parker J. Palmer is to seek "dis-illusionment," which in Palmer's vocabulary is a very good thing. After all, "no matter how difficult reality may be, it contains more life than any illusion."[3]

Palmer writes from the context of Quaker—and thus Christian— tradition, but his work has clear relevance for anyone interested in the care of the soul. If you are of a different religious tradition or no religious tradition at all, you will still find in this little book a spirituality that is not sectarian, does not flinch in the face of reality, will lead to insight, and will open up new vistas of possibility and promise for you—and through you, for your community.

How to Use this Book

Your 40-day journey with Parker J. Palmer gives you the opportunity to be mentored by a great contemporary spiritual writer and Christian leader. The purpose of the journey, however, is not just to gain "head knowledge" about Parker J. Palmer. Rather, it is to begin living what you learn.

You will probably benefit most by fixing a special time of day in which to "meet with" your spiritual mentor. It is easier to maintain a spiritual practice if you do it regularly at the same time. For many people, mornings, while the house is still quiet and before the busyness of the day begins, is a good time. Others will find that the noon hour or before bedtime serves well. We are all unique. Some of us are "morning people" and some of us are not. Do whatever works *for you* to maintain a regular meeting with Parker J. Palmer. Write it into your calendar and do your best to keep your appointments.

It is best if you complete your 40-day journey in forty days. A deepening focus and intensity of experience will be the result. However, it is certainly better to complete the journey than to give it up because you can't get it done in forty days. Indeed, making it a 40- or 20-week journey may better fit your schedule and it just might be that spending a whole week, or perhaps half a week, reflecting on the reading, the scripture, and the prayers, and then practicing what you are learning, could be a powerfully transforming experience as well. Again, set a schedule that works for you, only be consistent.

Each day of the journey begins with a reading from Parker J. Palmer. You will note that the readings, from day to day, build on each other and introduce you to key ideas in his understanding of Christian life and faith. Read each selection slowly, letting the words sink into your consciousness. You may want to read each selection two or three times before moving on, perhaps reading it out loud once.

Following the reading from Palmer's writings, you will find the heading *Biblical Wisdom* and a brief passage from the Bible that relates directly to what he has said. As with the selection from Palmer, read the biblical text slowly, letting the words sink into your consciousness.

Following the biblical reading, you will find the heading *Silence for Meditation.* Here you should take anywhere from five to twenty minutes meditating on the two readings. Begin by getting centered. Sit with your back straight, eyes closed, hands folded in your lap, and breathe slowly and deeply. Remember that breath is a gift of God; it is God's gift of life. Do nothing for two or three minutes other than simply observe your breath. Focus your awareness on the end of your nose. Feel the breath enter through your nostrils and leave through your nostrils.

Once you feel your mind and spirit settling down, open your eyes and read both the daily reading and the biblical text again. Read them slowly, focus on each word or phrase, savor them, explore possible meanings and implications. At the end of each day you will find a blank page with the heading *Notes.* As you meditate on the readings, jot down any insights that occur to you. Do the readings raise any questions for you? Write them down. Do the readings suggest anything you should do? Write it down.

Stay at it as long as it feels useful. When your mind is ready to move on, close your eyes and observe your breath for a minute or so. Then return to the book and the next heading: *Questions to Ponder.* Here you will find a few pointed questions by Henry French, the book's compiler and editor, on the day's reading. These are general questions intended for all spiritual seekers and communities of faith. Think them through and write your answers (and the implications of your answers for your own life of faith and for your community of faith) in the *Notes* section.

Many of these *Questions to Ponder* are designed to remind us—as Palmer would affirm—that although spirituality is always personal, it is simultaneously relational and communal. A number of the questions, therefore, apply the relevance of the day's reading to faith communities. Just remember, a faith community may be as large as a regular organized gathering of any religious tradition or as small as a family or the relationship between spiritual friends. You don't need to be a member of a church, synagogue, mosque, or temple to be part of a faith community. Answer the questions in the context of your particular faith community.

Then move on to the *Psalm Fragment.* Here you will find a brief verse or two from the Hebrew book of Psalms that relate to the day's reading. The Psalms have always been the mainstay of prayer in the Christian tradition and speak to the real situations in which we find ourselves—the kind of realism that Palmer's teaching and life resonate with.

Reflect for a moment on the *Psalm Fragment* and then continue on to the *Journal Reflections.* Several suggestions for journaling are given that apply the readings to your own personal experience. It is in journaling that the "day" reaches its climax, and the potential for transformative change is greatest. It would be best to buy a separate journal rather than use the *Notes* section of the book. For a journal you can use a spiral-bound or ring-bound notebook or one of the hardcover journal books sold in stationery stores. Below are some suggestions for how to keep a journal. For now, let's go back to the 40-day journey book.

The *Questions to Ponder* and *Journal Reflection* exercises are meant to assist you in reflecting on the daily reading and scripture quotations. Do not feel that you have to answer every question. You may choose which questions or exercises are most helpful to you. Sometimes a perfectly appropriate response to a question is, "I don't know" or "I'm not sure what I think about that." The important thing is to record your own thoughts and questions.

After *Journal Reflections*, you will find two more headings. The first is *Prayers of Hope & Healing*. One of the highest services a person of faith can perform is prayer for family and friends, for one's community of faith, for the victims of injustice, and for one's enemies. Under this heading you will find suggestions for prayer that relate to the key points in the day's readings. The last heading (before *Notes*) is *Prayer for Today*, a one- or two-line prayer to end your "appointment" with Parker J. Palmer, and to be prayed from time to time throughout the day.

HINTS ON KEEPING A JOURNAL

A journal is a very helpful tool. Keeping a journal is a form of meditation, a profound way of getting to know yourself—and God—more deeply. Although you could read your 40-day journey book and reflect on it "in your head," writing can help you focus your thoughts, clarify your thinking, and keep a record of your insights, questions, and prayers. Writing is generative: it enables you to have thoughts you would not otherwise have had.

A FEW HINTS FOR JOURNALING

1. Write in your journal with grace. Don't get stuck in trying to do it perfectly. Just write freely. Don't worry about literary style, spelling, or grammar. Your goal is simply to generate thoughts pertinent to your own life and get them down on paper.
2. You may want to begin and end your journaling with prayer. Ask for the guidance and wisdom of the Spirit (and thank God for that guidance and wisdom when you are done).
3. If your journaling takes you in directions that go beyond the journaling questions in your 40-day book, go there. Let the questions encourage, not limit, your writing.
4. Respond honestly. Don't write what you think you're supposed to believe. Write down what you really do believe, in so far as you can identify that. If you don't know, or are not sure, or if you have questions, record those. Questions are often openings to spiritual growth.
5. Carry your 40-day book and journal around with you every day during your journey (if only keep them safe from prying eyes). The 40-day journey process is an intense experience that doesn't stop when you close the book. Your mind and heart and spirit will be engaged all day, and it will be helpful to have your book and journal handy to take notes or make new entries as they occur to you.

JOURNEYING WITH OTHERS

You can use your 40-day book with another person, a spiritual friend or partner, or with a small group. It would be best for each person first do his or her own reading, reflection, and writing in solitude. Then when you come together, share the insights you have gained from your time alone. Your discussion will probably focus on the *Questions to Ponder,* however, if the relationship is intimate, you may feel comfortable sharing some of what you have written in your journal. No one, however, should ever be pressured to share anything in their journal if they are not comfortable doing so.

Remember that your goal is to learn from one another, not to argue, nor to prove that you are right and the other person wrong. Just practice listening and trying to understand why your partner, friend, or colleague thinks as he or she does.

Practicing intercessory prayer together, you will find, will strengthen the spiritual bonds of those who take the journey together. And as you all work to translate insight into action, sharing your experience with each other is a way of encouraging and guiding each other and provides the opportunity to provide feedback to each other gently if that becomes necessary.

CONTINUING THE JOURNEY

When the forty days (or forty weeks) are over, a milestone has been reached, but the journey needn't end. One goal of the 40-day series is to introduce you to a particular spiritual guide with the hope that, having whet your appetite, you will want to keep the journey going. At the end of the book are some suggestions for further reading that will take you deeper on your journey with your mentor.

WHO IS PARKER J. PALMER?

Parker J. Palmer was born on February 28, 1939, in Chicago. After graduating from Carleton College in Minnesota in 1961, he attended Union Theological Seminary in New York with an eye toward a vocation in Christian ministry. He soon discovered, however, that ordained ministry was not his passion, and he left New York, heading west to the University of California, Berkeley, where he earned a Ph.D. in sociology. In his own words, he was discovering that "teaching . . . is my native way of being in the world."[4]

While a student at Berkeley, Palmer taught for two years, confirming his love of teaching on the one hand, but discovering, on the other hand, that a university career was not what he was seeking. Leaving Berkeley in the late 1960s, Palmer headed back east, this time to Washington, D.C., where he became active in the demanding role of a community organizer. Then as now, peace and justice issues were bedrock concerns for Palmer and motivated him to take on the "urban crisis."

After two years spent learning the ropes as a community activist, Palmer was offered and accepted a position with Georgetown University to get students actively involved in the community. It proved a good position for a man who wanted to teach but needed a classroom without walls.

Five years of immersion in the intense and often conflicted realities of community organizing led to "burn-out" and a yearlong sabbatical at Pendle Hill, a Quaker learning and retreat center near Philadelphia. During his sabbatical, Palmer experienced new, more intimate dimensions of community and began learning *within community* to listen more intentionally and intently to his own inner teacher. The sabbatical evolved into a ten-year stay at Pendle Hill (1975–1985), where Palmer served variously as dean of studies, teacher, and writer-in-residence while learning more about the landscape of his own soul.

A teacher at heart (or perhaps it would be more correct to say a *teacher at soul*), Palmer spent years within institutions learning the painful, personal truth that to be himself he needed to work outside institutional structures. The conflicts and competition, the politics, and the compromises and constraints of institutional life were deadening rather than enlivening for him. Even gentler, more personal institutions like Pendle Hill, while providing a context for personal growth, were ultimately not the context where Palmer's true vocation could be fully realized.

The road Palmer traveled from Carleton College to Union Theological Seminary to the University of California and then through community organizing to Georgetown University and finally to Pendle Hill was a road littered with painfully stripped-away illusions as to who he is and what he is meant to do. He has learned the value and necessity of radical "dis-illusionment," of dismantling the cultural and personal illusions that keep us from discovering our true identity and from living authentically out of both our gifts and strengths and our limits and liabilities.

The task of replacing illusions with reality is arduous and painful, and for Palmer it included two descents into the darkness of depression during his forties.[5] His experiences of dis-illusionment and depression have led to a high degree of self-knowledge that undergirds his remarkable and highly regarded career as a teacher, consultant, writer, speaker, and social activist. Some ten years ago, Palmer founded the Center for Courage & Renewal, an organization that has, in his own words, "been putting wheels" on his ideas. After you have encountered the ideas of Parker J. Palmer, you might want to visit his Web site resources for continuing growth (www.CourageRenewal.org).

In *Let Your Life Speak,* a book of gentle but hard won wisdom, Palmer writes: "My gift as a teacher is the ability to "dance" with my students, to teach and learn with them through dialogue and interaction." *40-Day Journey with Parker J. Palmer* is your invitation to join him "in the dance of teaching and learning."[6]

40-DAY

Journey

WITH PARKER J. PALMER

Day 1

THE SPIRITUAL JOURNEY SHARPENS AND magnifies our sense of contradiction. And should it not be so? The wholeness of the Spirit contrasts dramatically with the brokenness of our persons and our world. The truth of the Spirit only highlights the untruths we are living. Indeed, the ultimate contradiction is the apparent opposition between God's light and our own shadowed lives.

For some of us the contrast between God and world is so great that we abandon the spiritual quest. We turn away from God's brilliance and walk in shadows because we do not wish to see ourselves in an unbecoming light. For others, the tension is resolved by disowning the dark world and trying to live in a bright but private realm. We hold the world at a distance and seek out situations which satisfy our need to stay "pure." In one way or another, we remove ourselves from the great dramas of life where God and world interact, where contradiction abounds.

But there is a third way to respond. A way beyond choosing either this pole or that. Let's call it "living the contradictions." Here we refuse to flee from tension but allow that tension to occupy the center of our lives. And why would anyone walk this difficult path? Because by doing so we may receive one of the great gifts of the spiritual life—*the transformation of contradiction into paradox.* The poles of either/or, the choices we thought we had to make, may become signs of a larger truth than we had even dreamed. And in that truth, our lives may become larger than we had ever imagined possible.

ↄ

BIBLICAL WISDOM

And this is the judgment, that the light has come into the world, and people loved darkness rather than light because their deeds were evil. . . . But those who do what is true come to the light, so that it may be clearly seen that their deeds have been done in God. John 3:19, 21

SILENCE FOR MEDITATION

QUESTIONS TO PONDER

- In your experience, does the spiritual journey both sharpen and magnify our sense of contradiction? Explain.
- In what ways does your community of faith help (or hinder) you in addressing, understanding, and creatively confronting the contrast between God and the world?
- How would you explain the difference between "contradiction" and "paradox"?

PSALM FRAGMENT

If I say, "Surely the darkness shall cover me,
and the light around me become night,"
even the darkness is not dark to you;
the night is as bright as the day,
for darkness is as light to you. Psalm 139:11-12

JOURNAL REFLECTIONS

- As you begin this 40-day journey with Parker J. Palmer, reflect in your journal on some of the "contradictions" that trouble and/or challenge you on your spiritual journey.
- Palmer writes: "The truth of the Spirit only highlights the untruths we are living." As you reflect on your life and relationships, are there any untruths you are living that the Spirit might be highlighting? Explain.
- What would it mean to you to begin living the contradictions in your personal, professional, and spiritual lives?

PRAYERS OF HOPE & HEALING

Pray for people you know who are struggling with "the apparent opposition between God's light and our own shadowed lives," that they might experience the reality of God's everywhere—and always-loving presence.

PRAYER FOR TODAY

Ever-loving and ever-present God, let me find you and follow you in both light and shadow today. Amen.

NOTES

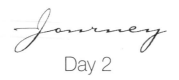

Day 2

LOREN EISELEY TELLS A STORY which helps me feel the power of recognizing life's contradictions. That great naturalist once spent time in a seaside town called Costabel and, plagued by lifelong insomnia, spent the early morning hours walking the beach. Each day at sunrise he found townspeople combing the sand for starfish which had washed ashore during the night, to kill them for commercial purposes. It was, for Eiseley, a sign, however small, of the ways the world says no to life.

But one morning Eiseley got up unusually early, and discovered a solitary figure on the beach. This man, too, was gathering starfish, but each time he found one alive, he would pick it up and throw it as far as he could out beyond the breaking surf, back to the nurturing ocean from which it came. . . .

Eiseley named this man "the star thrower," and in a moving meditation he writes of how this man and his pre-dawn work contradicted everything that Eiseley had been taught about evolution and the survival of the fittest. Here on the beach in Costabel the strong reached down to save, not crush, the weak. And Eiseley wonders: is there a star thrower at work in the universe, a God who contradicts death, a God whose nature (in the words of Thomas Merton) is "mercy within mercy within mercy"?

That story is rich in meaning for me. . . . It speaks of how ordinary men and women can participate in God's enveloping mercy.

֊

BIBLICAL WISDOM

But Jesus . . . said to him, "Go home to your friends, and tell them how much the Lord has done for you, and what mercy he has shown you." Mark 5:19

SILENCE FOR MEDITATION

Questions to Ponder

- What are some ways the world says no to life?
- Does your community of faith encourage (or hinder) you in saying yes to life and no to death? Is there more that could be done?
- Who are the "star throwers" in your experience? What qualities or character traits do they seem to have? Are they always appreciated? Why or why not?

Psalm Fragment

Answer me, O Lord, for your steadfast love is good;
according to your abundant mercy, turn to me. Psalm 69:16

Journal Reflections

- Write about your response to Eiseley's story. What emotions does it evoke? How do you react to the "star thrower"? Why?
- Reflect on yourself. To what degree are you a "star thrower"? In what ways do you "participate in God's enveloping mercy"?
- Journal about your image of God. Do you see God as one "whose nature . . . is 'mercy within mercy within mercy'"? How does your image of God help to shape your life and your response to others?

Prayers of Hope & Healing

Pray for people who are afraid of God and afraid of life, that they might richly experience God's yes to them and to life.

Prayer for Today

Holy God, let me be so open to your mercy today that it flows through me to others. Amen.

Notes

Day 3

WE LIVE IN A TIME of extreme self-consciousness, a time of self-doubt, self-examination, self-help. We seem aware of every inner perturbation, as if we had been born with inner seismographs capable of measuring each movement along our personal fault lines. Ours is a time in which health is supposed to come by focusing on ourselves and by seeking the resources for self-renewal.

But we've got it all backwards! For self-health is one of those strange things in human life which eludes those who aim directly at it, but comes to those who aim elsewhere. It was best said in the words of Jesus: "He who finds his life will lose it, and he who loses his life for my sake will find it." So we must learn, in this twisted age, that the ultimate therapy is to identify our own pain with the pain of others, and then band together to resist the conditions that create our common malady.

The ultimate therapy is to translate our private problems into public issues. In doing so we will discover that some of our private problems are too trivial to be dignified with public status, and they will fall away. But others, we will discover, are not private at all—they are common to our time. And as we learn to see our own plight in the lives of our brothers and sisters we will begin to find health. Therapy involves identifying and building communities of concern. Only so can we heal ourselves.

BIBLICAL WISDOM

No testing has overtaken you that is not common to everyone. 1 Corinthians 10:13a

SILENCE FOR MEDITATION

QUESTIONS TO PONDER

- What does it mean to identify our own pain with the pain of others? How might that be therapeutic?
- What would a community of faith that helped its people identify their own pain with the pain of others look like? In what ways would it be what Palmer calls a "community of concern"?
- In what way is it true that "as we learn to see our own plight in the lives of our brothers and sisters we will begin to find health"?

PSALM FRAGMENT

Happy are those who consider the poor;
*   the LORD delivers them in the day of trouble.* Psalm 41:1

JOURNAL REFLECTIONS

- Reflect on your life and relationships and then write about how you are doing in the area of self-health.
- As Palmer suggests, make a list of your "private problems" and then translate the list into "public issues."
- Which of your "private problems are too trivial to be dignified with public status" and which are "common to our time"? What conclusions can you draw from this exercise? Are any actions or change of focus suggested?

PRAYERS OF HOPE & HEALING

Pray for those who are so preoccupied and self-absorbed that they cannot see the joys and sorrows of the world around them, that they might be open to the experience of others.

PRAYER FOR TODAY

Healing God, help me to find my health in seeking the health of others. Amen.

NOTES

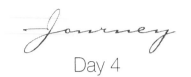

Day 4

MOST PEOPLE SEEM TO ASSUME that scarcity is a simple fact of life. How else can one explain the obsession with acquiring, consuming, and hoarding which permeates our society? We live in constant fear of the future—the fear that money will run out, that food supplies will dwindle, that housing will be unavailable. And as we act on those fears, the assumption becomes reality! As we consume more than we need, as we hoard against the future, then stores do dwindle and prices do rise and there will be too little to go around.

The tragic victims of this self-fulfilling prophecy are, of course, the "have-nots" of this world who lack the capital to act out their economic fears. For them, scarcity is no assumption at all: It is a hard and cruel fact of life. But that fact is created by people who have a choice—the choice to assume scarcity and grab for all one can get, or the choice to assume abundance and to live in such a way as to create and share it. For these people, for those of us who are affluent and educated—the matter of choosing assumptions is more than academic. Our souls and the lives of others hang in the balance.

BIBLICAL WISDOM

And do not keep striving for what you are to eat and what you are to drink, and do not keep worrying. For it is the nations of the world that strive after all these things, and your Father knows that you need them. Luke 12:29-30

SILENCE FOR MEDITATION

QUESTIONS TO PONDER

- Does it make sense to assume abundance rather than scarcity? Why or why not?
- What forces in our society encourage us to assume scarcity? Why?
- How might a community of faith help its members choose to operate out of assumptions of abundance?

PSALM FRAGMENT

How precious is your steadfast love, O God!
All people may take refuge in the shadow of your wings.
They feast on the abundance of your house,
and you give them drink from the river of your delights.
For with you is the fountain of life;
in your light we see light. Psalm 36:7-9

JOURNAL REFLECTIONS

- Examine your attitudes and actions. Do they reflect someone who assumes scarcity or abundance? Explain.
- Why does Palmer say that "our souls and the lives of others hang in the balance" depending upon whether we choose to assume scarcity or choose to assume abundance in the way we relate to the world?
- If you are living mostly under the assumption of scarcity, what steps might you begin taking to open you to the experience of abundance? If you are living mostly under the assumption of abundance, what has led you to this place?

PRAYERS OF HOPE & HEALING

Pray that those who have more than enough would be satisfied with just enough so that those who don't have enough might have enough.

PRAYER FOR TODAY

Gracious God, you have created a world where there is enough for everybody; let me never want more than enough until everyone has enough. Amen.

NOTES

Day 5

WHAT IS TRULY REMARKABLE ABOUT the human animal is not only that we take physical abundance and make it scarcity, but that we do the same with the infinite supply of goods of the Spirit. It is one thing to overvalue diamonds or undersupply tomatoes and find them scarce. It is quite another thing to treat love and affection and trust and regard as entities in short supply. And yet how many of us do exactly that? How often, in our relationships, do we act as if the stores of love were limited? . . . Is not this the basis of all human jealousies and envies, this instinct that there are not enough of these Spirit-goods to go around?

Or take a human good like pleasure or fun. Clearly the ways of having fun are infinite, limited only by our imaginations. But how many people spend weekends and summers resenting that they lack the money to *really* have fun—or that all the money they spent failed to buy enough of the product? We have limited the supply of "fun," and have put the power to "produce" it in the hands of sports promoters, casino operators, and travel agents. We have put ourselves in the position of anxious and impoverished consumers wanting to buy from the approved sources but with never enough cash or enough satisfaction to come out ahead. We have made that which is obviously abundant into that which is scarce.

⌒

BIBLICAL WISDOM

The fruit of the Spirit is love, joy, peace, patience, kindness, generosity, faithfulness, gentleness, and self-control. There is no law against such things. Galatians 5:22-23

SILENCE FOR MEDITATION

QUESTIONS TO PONDER

- What are the forces in our culture that want us to believe that the goods of the Spirit are limited and scarce? Why is it hard to resist these forces?

- In what ways has fun been turned into a commodity? How else might one view fun?
- In a consumerist and scarcity-driven society, how might people of faith demonstrate that the goods of the Spirit are both free and abundant?

PSALM FRAGMENT

I have not hidden your saving help within my heart,
I have spoken of your faithfulness and your salvation;
I have not concealed your steadfast love and your faithfulness
from the great congregation. Psalm 40:10

JOURNAL REFLECTIONS

- Make a list of the "Spirit-goods" that give joy, meaning, and purpose to your life.
- Reflect on your relationships. Do you act as if the stores of love were limited or unlimited? Explain. Any changes suggested?
- Write about the times, places, and people with whom you have real fun. How much does money have to do with this fun?

PRAYERS OF HOPE & HEALING

Pray for those who either feel unloved or who fear losing love, that they might experience both the steadfastness of God's love and faithful human love.

PRAYER FOR TODAY

Loving God, let me love and be loved today with the same freedom and abundance with which you love. Amen.

NOTES

Journey

Day 6

AS WE LOOK AT NATURE, at what is simply and freely given to us in creation, we cannot help but be impressed with its abundance. Properly treated, nature seems capable of infinite self-replenishment. Seeds grow in fertile soil; animals multiply apace; the soil is recreated by the death of flora and fauna; the earth is fecund beyond imagination. And what nature does not supply ready made, a humane technology is able to fabricate: amalgams and compounds and derivatives for meeting our every need. Set aside for the moment our misuse of the earth and the madness which has overtaken our technology, and simply contemplate the abundance of nature and human inventiveness, in its right order.

In the midst of such abundance how can we explain the scarcity assumption? Surrounded by a grace that seems capable of meeting reasonable human needs, how did we end up with things in short supply?

ᔉ

BIBLICAL WISDOM

And God is able to provide you with every blessing in abundance, so that by always having enough of everything, you may share abundantly in every good work. 2 Corinthians 9:8

SILENCE FOR MEDITATION

QUESTIONS TO PONDER

- How do you explain the scarcity assumption?
- What would be easier: to repudiate the scarcity assumption as an individual or as a member of a like-minded community? Why?
- Within your community of faith, how might you and others begin to challenge the scarcity assumption?

PSALM FRAGMENT

You cause the grass to grow for the cattle,
and plants for people to use,
to bring forth food from the earth,
and wine to gladden the human heart,
oil to make the face shine,
and bread to strengthen the human heart. Psalm 104:14-15

JOURNAL REFLECTIONS

- Meditate on the "grace that seems capable of meeting reasonable human needs." What feelings are evoked in you?
- Make a list of your reasonable human needs. Make a list of your "needs" that perhaps don't seem so reasonable any more.
- What steps might you take to, as Gandhi said, "live simply so that others might simply live"?

PRAYERS OF HOPE & HEALING

Pray that we might learn to take the gifts of nature (and nature's God) and add them to the fruits of a "humane technology" to make this world a good and trustworthy place for all.

PRAYER FOR TODAY

Holy God, today let me rejoice in simple things, in ordinary things, in the goods of the Spirit and the goods of the earth. Amen.

NOTES

Journey

Day 7

MOST OF US GAIN OUR sense of self not from what we share with others, but from the ways we are different from them. I define myself not in terms of what you and I have in common, but by what I have that you don't and what you have that I don't. I define myself in relation to scarcities which we possess unequally.

Somewhere deep within us, we fear commonality. We want to be unique, different, individual. We hardly notice those things in which we are similar, but we are sharply aware of those ways in which we are different. We know quickly the imbalances that exist between us—in wealth, and personality, and clothing, and education. When we meet, we instantly ask for evidence of our differences. What is your job? Where did you go to school? And behind it all is the weighing and the measuring, the assessment of who has more and who has less, the search for our distinctions. . . .

In theological terms, I am speaking here of the problem of idolatry. For by gaining identity from the possession of scarce goods, we are establishing those goods as gods in our lives. We give these gods the power to make us happy or miserable; the power to discriminate among people, separating the worthy from the unworthy, the better from the worse. By attaching our identity to that which only a few can have, we ignore the intrinsic preciousness of all human life. Worse still, we help maintain a social structure which gives some people an exaggerated sense of worth while discouraging others from ever feeling worthy at all.

BIBLICAL WISDOM

There is no longer Jew or Greek, there is no longer slave or free, there is no longer male and female; for all of you are one in Christ Jesus. Galatians 3:28

SILENCE FOR MEDITATION

QUESTIONS TO PONDER

- Do you agree with Palmer that "most of us gain our sense of self not from what we share with others, but from the ways we are different from them"? Explain.
- In what ways (and why) does our culture encourage us to fear commonality?
- How can people of faith challenge the idolatry that Palmer writes about?

PSALM FRAGMENT

For great is the LORD, and greatly to be praised;
*   he is to be revered above all gods.*
For all the gods of the peoples are idols,
*   but the LORD made the heavens.* Psalm 96:4-5

JOURNAL REFLECTIONS

- Reflect on yourself, and write about where you gain your sense of self.
- Reflect on yourself, and write about whether your sense of self-worth comes mostly from within yourself or from externals, for example, job, possessions, wealth, position, relationships, and so forth.
- Meditate on this: If all the externals in your life were taken away, who would you be?

PRAYERS OF HOPE & HEALING

Pray that all the distinctions we use to discriminate between and against people would melt away in the light of God's love that shows us all loved and lovely, all of great worth, all sisters and brothers.

PRAYER FOR TODAY

Ever-faithful, ever-loving God, let me live this day with no God but you. Amen.

NOTES

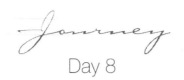

Day 8

TRUE ABUNDANCE COMES NOT TO those intent on securing wealth, but to those who are willing to share a life of apparent scarcity. Those who seek well-being, who grasp for more than their share, will find life pinched and fearful. They will reap only the anxiety of needing more, and the fear that someday it will all be taken away. But those who live in ways that allow others to live as well, those who reach out in service to their brothers and sisters with confidence that God will meet their needs, they will find a life of plenty which transcends the economics of scarcity.

Surely, this is a conversion. For in this spiritual wisdom, the world's logic is turned exactly upside down. Grasping brings less, and letting go brings more. What God wants from our fear of scarcity is not an obsessive capitalism, but the painful spiritual lesson that we cannot buy the security and identity we seek. Those will come to us only as we let go and live in the grace of God, and in solidarity with those for whom scarcity is not illusion but a matter of life and death.

BIBLICAL WISDOM

And he said to them, "Take care! Be on your guard against all kinds of greed; for one's life does not consist in the abundance of possessions." Luke 12:15

SILENCE FOR MEDITATION

QUESTIONS TO PONDER

- Does it seem counterintuitive to declare that "true abundance comes not to those intent on securing wealth, but to those who are willing to share a life of apparent scarcity"? Why or why not?
- How can you know if you are grasping for more than your share?
- How can you develop the confidence that God will meet your needs?

Psalm Fragment

Those who live at earth's farthest bounds are awed by your signs;
*   you make the gateways of the morning and the evening shout for joy.*
You visit the earth and water it,
*   you greatly enrich it;*
*   the river of God is full of water;*
*   you provide the people with grain,*
*   for so you have prepared it.* Psalm 65:8-9

Journal Reflections

- With respect to money and possessions, what would it mean to you to "let go and live in the grace of God"?
- Does the "spiritual wisdom" that "grasping brings less, and letting go brings more" make sense to you? Explain.
- List some ways in which you might live more "in solidarity with those for whom scarcity is not an illusion but a matter of life and death."

Prayers of Hope & Healing

Pray for those who are considering ways to live both more simply and more in solidarity with those who live in poverty, that their convictions might give them the courage to take action.

Prayer for Today

Holy God grant me to live this day with such trust in your care that I am free to care for others. Amen.

Notes

Day 9

UNDERLYING ALL MUST BE THE foundation of the spiritual life—prayer. I do not mean "saying prayers," which often means little more than special pleading that God grant me some seemingly scarce resource before my neighbor gets it. No, I mean by prayer a life that returns constantly to that silent, solitary place within, where God is met and where the abundance of life becomes manifest. . . .

A life of prayer is one in which we know the need to return constantly to a place removed, a place where the claims of the world can fall away and be seen for the illusions they are. This is the heart of prayer—the journey from illusion to truth. And of all the illusions we must contend with, the illusion of scarcity is one of the most important. As we settle into a deep listening for God's word, how ludicrous seem the grasping ways of daily life! In that silence and solitude with God, how clear it seems that "letting go" is the only thing to do, for we cannot hang on anyway! In prayer, the world's version of abundance is clearly seen as a snare and a delusion, while God's promise of abundance is perceived not as a future possibility but as reality, now.

BIBLICAL WISDOM

And whenever you pray, do not be like the hypocrites; for they love to stand and pray in the synagogues and at the street corners, so that they may be seen by others. Truly I tell you, they have received their reward. But whenever you pray, go into your room and shut the door and pray to your Father who is in secret; and your Father who sees in secret will reward you. Matthew 6:5-6

SILENCE FOR MEDITATION

QUESTIONS TO PONDER

- How might a community of faith provide its people with "a place removed, a place where the claims of the world can fall away and be seen for the illusions they are"?

- Do you agree that the world's vision of abundance is a snare and a delusion? Why or why not?
- In what ways is God's promise of abundance not a future possibility but a present reality?

PSALM FRAGMENT

For God alone my soul waits in silence. Psalm 62:1a

JOURNAL REFLECTIONS

- Write several paragraphs describing your prayer life. When do you pray? For whom or for what? How do you pray? Is prayer a source of strength or a source of frustration for you? Is there anything you would like to learn about prayer or any changes you would like to make in your prayer life?
- In what ways have you found prayer to be a journey from illusion to truth?
- Write about the place of silence and solitude in your life.

PRAYERS OF HOPE & HEALING

Pray for your community of faith, that it may be a place where prayer is learned and practiced and thus a place where illusion gives way to truth.

PRAYER FOR TODAY

Holy One, let me be still today and know that you are God. Amen.

NOTES

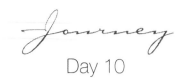

Day 10

MY KNOWLEDGE OF THE DIVIDED life comes first from personal experience: I yearn to be whole but dividedness often seems the easier choice. A "still small voice" speaks the truth about me, my work, or the world. I hear it and yet act as if I did not. I withhold a personal gift that might serve a good end or commit myself to a project I do not really believe in. I keep silent on an issue I should address or actively break faith with one of my own convictions. . . .

The divided life comes in many and varied forms. To cite just a few examples, it is the life we lead when:

- We refuse to invest ourselves in our work, diminishing its quality and distancing ourselves from those it is meant to serve.
- We make our living at jobs that violate our basic values, even when survival does not absolutely demand it.
- We remain in settings or relationships that steadily kill off our spirits.
- We harbor secrets to achieve personal gain at the expense of other people.
- We hide our beliefs from those who disagree with us to avoid conflict, challenge, and change.
- We conceal our true identities for fear of being criticized, shunned, or attacked.

⌒

BIBLICAL WISDOM

And whatever you do, in word or deed, do everything in the name of the Lord Jesus, giving thanks to God the Father through him. Colossians 3:17

SILENCE FOR MEDITATION

QUESTIONS TO PONDER

- Do you agree that what Palmer calls "the divided life" is a troubling reality for most if not all of us? Why or why not?
- In what ways (and why) does society encourage us to lead divided lives?
- How might people of faith learn to hear the "still small voice" that speaks the truth about us?

PSALM FRAGMENT

Teach me your way, O LORD,
*   that I may walk in your truth;*
*   give me an undivided heart to revere your name.* Psalm 86:11

JOURNAL REFLECTIONS

- Palmer's knowledge of the "divided life" came "first from personal experience." In what if any ways has your personal experience taught you about the divided life?
- Reread the bullet list in today's reading of some of the "many and varied forms" the divided life comes in. Which of them speak to your own experience? Explain.
- Meditate on what an undivided life would look like and feel like for you.

PRAYERS OF HOPE & HEALING

Pray for those for whom the divided life is a daily reality, that they might experience the wonder of knowing who they are and being who they are.

PRAYER FOR TODAY

Gracious God, you made me, love and value me; today grant me grace and courage to be me. Amen.

NOTES

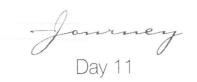

Day 11

As we become more obsessed with succeeding, or at least surviving, in that (so-called real) world, we lose touch with our souls and disappear into our roles . . . at considerable cost to self, to others, and to the world at large. It is a cost that can be itemized in ways well known to many of us:

- We sense that something is missing in our lives and search the world for it, not understanding that what is missing is us.
- We feel fraudulent, even invisible, because we are not in the world as who we really are.
- The light within us cannot illuminate the world's darkness.
- The darkness that is within us cannot be illuminated by the world's light.
- We project our inner darkness on others, making "enemies" of them and making the world a more dangerous place.
- Our inauthenticity and projections make real relationships impossible, leading to loneliness.
- Our contributions to the world—especially through the work we do—are tainted by duplicity and deprived of the life-giving energies of true self.

Those are not exactly the marks of a life well lived.

⌒

Biblical Wisdom

Who is wise and understanding among you? Show by your good life that your works are done with gentleness born of wisdom. James 3:13

Silence for Meditation

Questions to Ponder

- Why does Palmer say that our obsession "with succeeding, or at least surviving" comes at "considerable cost" not only to ourselves, but "to others, and to the world at large" as well?
- What does it mean to "lose touch with our souls and disappear into our roles"?
- What needs to be done to bring our souls and our roles into greater harmony?

Psalm Fragment

O Lord, all my longing is known to you;
my sighing is not hidden from you.
My heart throbs, my strength fails me;
as for the light of my eyes—it also has gone from me. Psalm 38:9-10

Journal Reflections

- Meditate on the degree of harmony between your soul and your roles.
- To what degree are you in the world as who you really are? Explain.
- Where in your life (doing what? with whom?) do you experience "the life-giving energies of true self"?

Prayers of Hope & Healing

Pray for those who are "obsessed with succeeding," that their understanding of success might become crafting a life of harmony between their souls and their roles.

Prayer for Today

Guiding God, today my life will express greater harmony between who I am and what I do. Amen.

Notes

Day 12

THE DIVIDED LIFE MAY BE endemic, but wholeness is always a choice. Once I have seen my dividedness, do I continue to live a contradiction— or do I try to bring my inner and outer worlds back into harmony?

"Being whole" is a self-evident good, so the answer would seem to be clear. And yet, as we all know, it is not. Time after time we choose against wholeness by slipping into a familiar pattern of evasion.

- First comes denial: surely what I have seen about myself cannot be true.
- Next comes equivocation: the inner voice speaks softly, and truth is a subtle, slippery thing, so how can I be sure of what my soul is saying?
- Next comes fear: if I let that inner voice dictate the shape of my life, what price might I have to pay in a world that sometimes punishes authenticity?
- Next comes cowardice: the divided life may be destructive, but at least I know the territory, while what lies beyond it is *terra incognita.*
- Then comes avarice: in some situations, I am rewarded for being willing to stifle my soul.

This pattern of self-evasion is powerful and persistent.

BIBLICAL WISDOM

I do not understand my own actions. For I do not do what I want, but I do the very thing I hate. Romans 7:15

SILENCE FOR MEDITATION

QUESTIONS TO PONDER

- If being whole is a self-evident good, why do so many choose against wholeness?
- Given the pattern of self-evasion that Palmer describes, how does one move toward genuine self-understanding?
- In what ways does the world sometimes punish authenticity?

PSALM FRAGMENT

Who are they that fear the LORD?
  He will teach them the way that they should choose. Psalm 25:12

JOURNAL REFLECTIONS

- Palmer writes that "wholeness is always a choice." In what ways are you aware of choosing wholeness in your life and relationships?
- Write about the spiritual practices that help you bring your "inner and outer worlds back into harmony."
- Do you have a *truth-teller* in your life, someone who can help you avoid the "pattern of self-evasion" that Palmer writes about? If so, write about your *truth-teller* and how he or she helps you to be honest with yourself. If not, where might you find such a person?

PRAYERS OF HOPE & HEALING

Pray for those whose "inner and outer worlds" are disharmonious, that they may find peace and hope in true self-knowledge.

PRAYER FOR TODAY

Holy One, today—following your word—I will seek in all that I do to choose life. Amen.

NOTES

Journey

Day 13

HOW DOES THE DIVIDED SELF become whole? "How to do it" questions are commonplace in our pragmatic culture, and so are the mechanistic answers they often evoke: "Here is a ten-step program you can pursue in the privacy of your own home—or on the flight between JFK and LAX—to achieve an undivided life. Do these exercises and your life will be transformed!"

Solutions of that sort are snake oil, of course. The quick-fix mentality that dominates our impatient world serves only to distract us from the lifelong journey toward wholeness. And the self-help methods so popular in our time, the best of which offer us support for that journey, sometimes reinforce the great American illusion that we can forever go it alone.

Of course, solitude is essential to personal integration: there are places in the landscapes of our lives where no one can accompany us. But because we are communal creatures who need each other's support—and because, left to our own devices, we have an endless capacity for self-absorption and self-deception—community is equally essential to rejoining soul and role. . . .

That kind of community—one that knows how to welcome the soul and help us hear its voice—I call a "circle of trust."

BIBLICAL WISDOM

Many proclaim themselves loyal,
but who can find one worthy of trust? Proverbs 20:6

SILENCE FOR MEDITATION

QUESTIONS TO PONDER

- In what ways would you (or would you not) describe your faith community as a "circle of trust"?

- What are the implications of saying that the "journey toward wholeness" is a "lifelong journey"?
- Should the journey toward wholeness be a solitary journey or one traveled with others? Explain.

PSALM FRAGMENT

How very good and pleasant it is
*   when kindred live together in unity! . . .*
For there the LORD ordained his blessing,
*   life forevermore.* Psalm 133:1, 3b

JOURNAL REFLECTIONS

- Are you impatient and looking for a quick fix, or patient and willing to go the distance on the journey toward wholeness? Explain.
- Who are the people in your life who know how to welcome your soul and help you hear its voice?
- What do your prefer more—solitude or community? Explain.

PRAYERS OF HOPE & HEALING

Pray for those who are lonely and disheartened on life's journey, that they may find loving and supportive community.

PRAYER FOR TODAY

Loving God, may I balance my needs for solitude and community today, taking time to be alone and time to be together. Amen.

NOTES

Journey

Day 14

THE CIRCLES OF TRUST I experienced at Pendle Hill (a Quaker study and retreat center) are a rare form of community—one that supports rather than supplants the individual quest for integrity—that is rooted in two basic beliefs. First, we all have an inner teacher whose guidance is more reliable than anything we can get from a doctrine, ideology, collective belief system, institution, or leader. Second, we all need other people to invite, amplify, and help us discern the inner teacher's voice for at least three reasons:

- The journey toward inner truth is too taxing to be made solo; lacking support, the solitary traveler soon becomes weary or fearful and is likely to quit the road.
- The path is too deeply hidden to be traveled without company: finding our way involves clues that are subtle and sometimes misleading, requiring the kind of discernment that can happen only in dialogue.
- The destination is too daunting to be achieved alone: we need community to find the courage to venture into the alien lands to which the inner teacher may call us.

BIBLICAL WISDOM

They devoted themselves to the apostles' teaching and fellowship, to the breaking of bread and the prayers. . . . All who believed were together and had all things in common; they would sell their possessions and goods and distribute the proceeds to all, as any had need. Day by day, as they spent much time together in the temple, they broke bread at home and ate their food with glad and generous hearts, praising God and having the goodwill of all the people. Acts 2:42, 44-47a

SILENCE FOR MEDITATION

Questions to Ponder

- Do you agree with Palmer that "we all have an inner teacher whose guidance is more reliable than anything we can get from a doctrine, ideology, collective belief system, institution, or leader"? Why or why not?
- Why might an organized community of faith be threatened by the notion of an "inner teacher"?
- Do you experience your faith community as aiding or hindering you in listening to your inner teacher?

Psalm Fragment

Good and upright is the LORD;
  therefore he instructs sinners in the way.
He leads the humble in what is right,
  and teaches the humble his way. Psalm 25:8-9

Journal Reflections

- Have you experienced your inner teacher? If so, write about the experience and its impact on you. If not, can you imagine having such an experience? How might you begin (or continue) to listen to your inner teacher?
- How important (or unimportant) are doctrine, ideology, collective belief systems, institutions, or leaders in your quest for wholeness and integrity? Explain.
- How comfortable (or uncomfortable) are you with the thought of needing other people "to invite, amplify, and help [you] discern the inner teacher's voice"?

Prayers of Hope & Healing

Pray for those who have difficulty trusting themselves to others, that they might be blessed with trustworthy friends for the journey toward wholeness.

Prayer for Today

Creator God, today I will listen as well as I can to the inner voice you created within me. Amen.

Notes

"NOBODY KNOWS WHAT THE SOUL is," says the poet Mary Oliver; "it comes and goes/like the wind over the water."[7] But just as we can name the functions of the wind, so we can name some of the functions of the soul without presuming to penetrate its mystery:

- The soul wants to keep us rooted in the ground of our own being, resisting the tendency of other faculties, like the intellect and the ego, to uproot us from who we are.
- The soul wants to keep us connected to the community in which we find life, for it understands that relationships are necessary if we are to thrive.
- The soul wants to tell us the truth about ourselves, our world, and the relation between the two, whether that truth is easy or hard to hear.
- The soul wants to give us life and wants us to pass that gift along, to become life-givers in a world that deals too much death.

All of us arrive on earth with souls in perfect form. But from the moment of birth onward, the soul or true self is assailed by deforming forces from without and within: by racism, sexism, economic injustice, and other social cancers; by jealousy, resentment, self-doubt, fear, and other demons of the inner life.

BIBLICAL WISDOM

Then you will understand righteousness and justice
and equity, every good path;
for wisdom will come into your heart,
and knowledge will be pleasant to your soul;
prudence will watch over you;
and understanding will guard you. Proverbs 2:9-11

SILENCE FOR MEDITATION

QUESTIONS TO PONDER

- Compare Palmer's description of the functions of the soul with what your faith tradition has taught you about the soul. In what ways are they the same or different?
- What, if any, other functions of the soul occur to you?
- What are some of the other social cancers and demons of the inner life that deform the soul?

PSALM FRAGMENT

As a deer longs for flowing streams,
*   so my soul longs for you, O God.*
My soul thirsts for God,
*   for the living God.* Psalm 42:1-2a

JOURNAL REFLECTIONS

- Write about your understanding of your soul. Do you agree with Palmer that "all of us arrive on earth with souls in perfect form"? Why or why not?
- What are the particular inner demons and social cancers that deform your soul? What might you do to more actively resist these deforming forces?
- What are the particular inner strengths and external forces that work to re-form your soul? What might you do to more actively cooperate with these reforming forces?

PRAYERS OF HOPE & HEALING

Pray for our society, that its soul-destroying forces might be restrained and its soul-strengthening forces enhanced.

PRAYER FOR TODAY

Creator God, my soul longs for you; let the longing of my soul be satisfied. Amen.

NOTES

Day 16

ALL OF THE GREAT SPIRITUAL traditions want to awaken us to the fact that we cocreate the reality in which we live. And all of them ask two questions intended to keep us awake: What are we sending from within ourselves out into the world, and what impact is it having "out there"? What is the world sending back at us, and what impact is it having "in here"? We are continually engaged in the evolution of self and world—and we have the power to choose, moment by moment, between that which gives life and that which deals death.

BIBLICAL WISDOM

I call heaven and earth to witness against you today that I have set before you life and death, blessings and curses. Choose life so that you and your descendants may live. Deuteronomy 30:19

SILENCE FOR MEDITATION

QUESTIONS TO PONDER

- What does it mean to say that "we cocreate the reality in which we live"?
- In what ways would a person who is "awake" to his or her cocreative role be and act differently than someone who is "asleep" to this reality?
- Does the notion that we cocreate the reality in which we live give rise to optimism or pessimism, hope or cynicism? Explain.

PSALM FRAGMENT

When I look at your heavens, the work of your fingers,
    the moon and the stars that you have established;
    what are human beings that you are mindful of them,
    mortals that you care for them?
Yet you have made them a little lower than God,
    and crowned them with glory and honor. Psalm 8:3-5

Journal Reflections

- If it is true that we cocreate the reality we live in, then it is important to know what kind of reality we want to live in. Write about the kind of reality you desire for yourself and others.
- Make a list of the attitudes and behaviors that would strengthen your ability to be a cocreator of the reality you desire for yourself and others.
- In what ways do you (or do you not) exercise "the power to choose, moment by moment, between that which gives life and that which deals death"?

Prayers of Hope & Healing

Pray that we would all "awaken . . . to the fact that we cocreate the reality in which we live," and that, having awakened, we would work together to create a society where people choose life rather than deal death.

Prayer for Today

God of life, as I move through this day, may my choices reflect a deep reverence for life. Amen.

Notes

WHEN WE SPLIT SOLITUDE AND community into an either-or and act as if we can get along with only one or the other, we put ourselves in spiritual peril. The theologian Dietrich Bonhoeffer warned us about this risk in his classic *Life Together:* "Let [the person] who cannot be alone beware of community. Let the [person] who is not in community beware of being alone."[8]

Bonhoeffer's warning is based on two simple truths. We have much to learn from within, but it is easy to get lost in the labyrinth of the inner life. We have much to learn from others, but it is easy to get lost in the confusion of the crowd. So we need solitude and community simultaneously: what we learn in one mode can check and balance what we learn in the other. Together they make us whole, like breathing in and breathing out. . . .

If we are to hold solitude and community together as a true paradox, we need to deepen our understanding of both poles. *Solitude* does not necessarily mean living apart from others; rather it means never living apart from one's self. It is not about the absence of other people—it is about being fully present to ourselves, whether or not we are with others. *Community* does not necessarily mean living face-to-face with others; rather, it means never losing the awareness that we are connected to each other. It is not about the presence of other people—it is about being fully open to the reality of relationship, whether or not we are alone.

BIBLICAL WISDOM

And let us consider how to provoke one another to love and good deeds, not neglecting to meet together, as is the habit of some, but encouraging one another. Hebrews 10:24-25a

SILENCE FOR MEDITATION

Questions to Ponder

- What does it mean to never live apart from oneself, even when with others?
- What does it mean to never lose the awareness that we are connected to each other, even when we are alone?
- In what ways does your community of faith encourage and support your need for both solitude and community?

Psalm Fragment

I commune with my heart in the night;
  I meditate and search my spirit. Psalm 77:6

Journal Reflections

- Write about how you use solitude to learn from within and what you are learning from solitude.
- Write about how you learn from others and what you are learning from participating in community.
- Do you feel that you are fully present to yourself whether or not you are with others? Why or why not? What might you have to do to be more fully present to yourself at times when you are alone and at times when you are with others?

Prayers of Hope & Healing

Pray that everyone in your faith community might learn to balance their needs for both solitude and community and that they might support each other in this effort.

Prayer for Today

God of silence and song, today I will be fully present *to* myself and fully present *as* myself to others. Amen.

Notes

Day 18

"ASK ME WHETHER WHAT I have done is my life."[9] For some those words will be nonsense, nothing more than a poet's loose way with language and logic. Of course what I have done is my life! To what am I supposed to compare it? But for others, and I am one, the poet's words will be precise, piercing, and disquieting. They remind me of moments when it is clear—if I have eyes to see—that the life I am living is not the life that wants to live in me. In those moments, I sometimes catch a glimpse of my true life, a life hidden like the river beneath the ice. And in the spirit of the poet, I wonder: What am I meant to do? Who am I meant to be?

BIBLICAL WISDOM

And all of us, with unveiled faces, seeing the glory of the Lord as though reflected in a mirror, are being transformed into the same image from one degree of glory to another; for this comes from the Lord, the Spirit. 2 Corinthians 3:18

SILENCE FOR MEDITATION

QUESTIONS TO PONDER

- If you were asked whether what you have done is your life, how would you answer? Why?
- What are some of the ways in which we can live a life that is not ours?
- How does your faith community encourage (or hinder) you in living authentically and with integrity?

Psalm Fragment

For it was you who formed my inward parts;
   you knit me together in my mother's womb.
I praise you, for I am fearfully and wonderfully made.
   Wonderful are your works;
   that I know very well. . . .
In your book were written
   all the days that were formed for me,
   when none of them as yet existed. Psalm 139:13-14, 16b

Journal Reflections

- Write your answer to the question: "Who am I meant to be?"
- Write your answer to the question: "What am I meant to do?"
- What might you need to do to begin being more of who you are meant to be and to begin doing more of what you are meant to do?

Prayers of Hope & Healing

Pray that in all your relationships you would encourage others to be who they are and do what they were meant to do.

Prayer for Today

Holy One, may I do nothing today that violates my true self. Amen.

Notes

Day 19

VOCATION DOES NOT COME FROM willfulness. It comes from listening. I must listen to my life and try to understand what it is truly about— quite apart from what I would like it to be about—or my life will never represent anything real in the world, no matter how earnest my intentions.

That insight is hidden in the word *vocation* itself, which is rooted in the Latin for "voice." *Vocation* does not mean a goal that I pursue. It is a calling that I hear. Before I can tell my life what I want to do with it, I must listen to my life telling me who I am. I must listen for the truths and values at the heart of my own identity, not the standards by which I *must* live—but the standards by which I cannot help but live if I am living my own life.

Behind this understanding of vocation is a truth that the ego does not want to hear because it threatens the ego's turf: everyone has a life that is different from the "I" of daily consciousness, a life that is trying to live through the "I" who is its vessel. This is what the poet knows and what every wisdom tradition teaches: there is a great gulf between the way my ego wants to identify me, with its protective masks and self-serving fictions, and my true self.

ə

BIBLICAL WISDOM

However that may be, let each of you lead the life that the Lord has assigned, to which God called you. 1 Corinthians 7:17

SILENCE FOR MEDITATION

QUESTIONS TO PONDER

- How do you "listen to [your] life and try to understand what it is truly about"?
- In what ways does it (or doesn't it) make sense to think about *vocation* as a "calling" rather than a "goal"?
- What social pressures are there that work against our accepting *vocation* as a calling?

PSALM FRAGMENT

O LORD, you have searched me and known me.
You know when I sit down and when I rise up;
*   you discern my thoughts from far away.*
You search out my path and my lying down,
*   and are acquainted with all my ways.* Psalm 139:1-3

JOURNAL REFLECTIONS

- Who does the "I" of daily consciousness (the ego) want you to be? How does this match up with what you think your life is truly about?
- Write about the truths and values at the heart of your identity.
- To what degree do your job, relationships, and other activities reflect the truths and values at the heart of your identity?

PRAYERS OF HOPE & HEALING

Pray for those whose ego masks their true self, that they might find the courage to listen to their life and begin to live it.

PRAYER FOR TODAY

Loving God, today I will listen to my life; may I be fearless and honest in my listening. Amen.

NOTES

Day 20

BUT IF I AM TO let my life speak things I want to hear, things I would gladly tell others, I must also let it speak things I do not want to hear and would never tell anyone else! My life is not only about my strengths and virtues; it is also about my liabilities and my limits, my trespasses and my shadow. An inevitable though often ignored dimension of the quest for "wholeness" is that we must embrace what we dislike or find shameful about ourselves as well as what we are confident or proud of. That is why the poet says, "ask me mistakes I have made."[10]

BIBLICAL WISDOM

If we say that we have no sin, we deceive ourselves, and the truth is not in us.
1 John 1:8

SILENCE FOR MEDITATION

QUESTIONS TO PONDER

- What does it mean to let my life "speak things I do not want to hear and would never tell anyone else"?
- Why does the quest for wholeness require us to "embrace what we dislike or find shameful about ourselves"?
- Is your community of faith a safe place for you to be honest about your liabilities and your limits, your trespasses and your shadow? Explain.

PSALM FRAGMENT

While I kept silence, my body wasted away
through my groaning all day long. . . .
Then I acknowledged my sin to you,
and I did not hide my iniquity. Psalm 32:3, 5

Journal Reflections

- What are some of the things that you "do not want to hear [about your-self] and would never tell anyone else"? What would it mean to embrace these things?
- Do you have a confidant, someone you can talk to about your liabilities, limits, trespasses, and shadow? If so, how does the experience help your quest for wholeness? If not, what steps could you take to find such a person?
- If someone were to ask you what mistakes you have made, what would you say?

Prayers of Hope & Healing

Pray for those who listen to others speak about what they "dislike or find shameful" about themselves, that they would not judge, but listen with compassion.

Prayer for Today

Forgiving God, I will not hide my liabilities, limits, trespasses, and shadow from myself or from you. Amen.

Notes

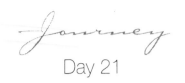

Day 21

THE GOD WHOM I KNOW dwells quietly in the root system of the very nature of things. This is the God who, when asked by Moses for a name, responded, "I AM WHO I AM" (Exodus 3:14), an answer that has less to do with the moral rules for which Moses made God famous than with elemental "isness" and selfhood. If, as I believe, we are all made in God's image, we could all give the same answer when asked who we are: "I Am who I Am." One dwells with God by being faithful to one's nature. One crosses God by trying to be something one is not. Reality—including one's own—is divine, to be not defied but honored.

BIBLICAL WISDOM

So God created humankind in his image,
in the image of God he created them;
male and female he created them. Genesis 1:27

SILENCE FOR MEDITATION

QUESTIONS TO PONDER

- How does your faith community talk about where God dwells?
- Does it change how you think about God to picture God as one who "dwells quietly in the root system of the very nature of things"? How or why not?
- What does it mean to say that we are all made in God's image?

PSALM FRAGMENT

Be still, and know that I am God! Psalm 46:10a

Journal Reflections

- Meditate on the expression "I Am who I Am" as an expression for who you are. What does it imply about you? Does it work for you? Why or why not?
- Reflect on Palmer's statement that "reality—including one's own—is divine, to be not defied but honored." What do you think he means? Do you agree with him? Why or why not? What would the implications be for how you think about (and respond to) reality—including your own?
- Make a list of the ways you are "faithful" to your own nature; make another list of ways you are "trying to be something [you are] not." Compare them. Any conclusions suggest themselves? Any things you need to do (or not do)?

Prayers of Hope & Healing

Pray for all those who have low self-esteem and self-worth, that they would experience the wonder and mystery of being made in the image of God.

Prayer for Today

Sustaining God, you who created me in your own image, may I reflect your image in all of my relationships. Amen.

Notes

Day 22

As often happens on the spiritual journey, we have arrived at the heart of a paradox: each time a door closes, the rest of the world opens up. All we need to do is stop pounding on the door that just closed, turn around—which puts the door behind us—and welcome the largeness of life that now lies open to our souls. The door that closed kept us from entering a room, but what now lies before us is the rest of reality. . . .

If we are to live our lives fully and well, we must learn to embrace the opposites, to live in a creative tension between our limits and our potentials. We must honor our limitations in ways that do not distort our nature, and we must trust and use our gifts in ways that fulfill the potentials God gave us. We must take the no of the way that closes and find the guidance it has to offer—and take the yes of the way that opens and respond with the yes of our lives.

BIBLICAL WISDOM

This one thing I do: forgetting what lies behind and straining forward to what lies ahead, I press on toward the goal for the prize of the heavenly call of God in Christ Jesus. Philippians 3:13b-14

SILENCE FOR MEDITATION

QUESTIONS TO PONDER

- Do you agree with Palmer that "each time a door closes, the rest of the world opens up"? Explain.
- When a door closes on us, why do we have the tendency to keep pounding on it rather than "welcome the largeness of life that now lies open to our souls"?
- In what ways might a door that has closed have guidance to offer us?

PSALM FRAGMENT

I kept my faith, even when I said,
"I am greatly afflicted." Psalm 116:10

JOURNAL REFLECTIONS

- How do you usually respond when face to face with a NO? Have you ever experienced a yes hidden within a no? Explain.
- Write about some experiences you have had of doors closing. At the time did you sense the rest of the world opening up for you?
- Are you a "cup half empty" or "cup half full" sort of person? Explain.

PRAYERS OF HOPE & HEALING

Pray for all who have been disappointed, that they might experience the "largeness of life" that lies open before them.

PRAYER FOR TODAY

God of all newness, if I run into a closed door today, let me find the yes hidden in the no. Amen.

NOTES

I NOW (AFTER THE EXPERIENCE of severe depression) know myself to be a person of weakness and strength, liability and giftedness, darkness and light. I now know that to be whole means to reject none of it but to embrace all of it.

Some may say that this embrace is narcissistic, an obsession with self at the expense of others, but that is not how I experience it. When I ignored my own truth on behalf of a distorted ego and ethic, I led a false life that caused others pain—for which I can only ask forgiveness. When I started attending to my own truth, more of that truth became available in my work and my relationships. I know now that anything one can do on behalf of true self is done ultimately in the service of others.

Others may say that "embracing one's wholeness" is just fancy talk for permission to sin, but again my experience is to the contrary. To embrace weakness, liability, and darkness as part of who I am gives that part less sway over me, because all it ever wanted was to be acknowledged as part of my whole self.

BIBLICAL WISDOM

So, I will boast all the more gladly of my weaknesses, so that the power of Christ may dwell in me. Therefore I am content with weaknesses, insults, hardships, persecutions, and calamities for the sake of Christ; for whenever I am weak, then I am strong. 2 Corinthians 12:9b-10

SILENCE FOR MEDITATION

QUESTIONS TO PONDER

- Do you think that embracing one's wholeness is just fancy talk for permission to sin? Why or why not?
- How would you describe the relationship between attending to your own truth and being truly available to serve others?

- In what ways (and for what purpose) might a distorted ego and ethic cause you to ignore your own truth?

PSALM FRAGMENT

Be gracious to me, O LORD, for I am in distress;
my eye wastes away from grief,
my soul and body also.
For my life is spent with sorrow,
and my years with sighing;
my strength fails because of my misery,
and my bones waste away. Psalm 31:9-10

JOURNAL REFLECTIONS

- It took the experience of severe depression for Palmer to come to know himself as "a person of weakness and strength, liability and giftedness, darkness and light." Write about any experiences you have had that have given you greater insight into your own truth.
- What would it mean to you to embrace weakness, liability, and darkness as part of who you are?
- What would it *feel like* to embrace weakness, liability, and darkness as part of who you are?

PRAYERS OF HOPE & HEALING

Pray that we all might have the courage to look into the mirror, see what is really there, and embrace ourselves with love and compassion.

PRAYER FOR TODAY

Loving God, as much as I can, today I am going to acknowledge and own the truth about myself and simply be who I am. Amen.

NOTES

Day 24

"LEADERSHIP" IS A CONCEPT WE often resist. It seems immodest, even self-aggrandizing, to think of ourselves as leaders. But if it is true that we are made for community, then leadership is everyone's vocation, and it can be an evasion to insist that it is not. When we live in the close-knit ecosystem called community, everyone follows and everyone leads.

Even I—a person who is unfit to be president of anything, who once galloped away from institutions on a high horse—have come to understand that for better or for worse, I lead by word and deed *simply because I am here doing what I do.* If you are also here, doing what you do, then you also exercise leadership of some sort.

BIBLICAL WISDOM

So then, whenever we have an opportunity, let us work for the good of all, and especially for those of the family of faith. Galatians 6:10

SILENCE FOR MEDITATION

QUESTIONS TO PONDER

- Define—and give examples of—leadership.
- In what ways is it true that leadership is everyone's vocation?
- What insights into the nature of community come from describing community as a close-knit ecosystem?

PSALM FRAGMENT

Let me hear of your steadfast love in the morning,
for in you I put my trust.
Teach me the way I should go,
for to you I lift up my soul. Psalm 143:8

Journal Reflections

- Do you see yourself as a leader or not? Explain.
- If in a community everyone follows and everyone leads, make a list of the ways you follow and the ways you lead in your faith community.
- Palmer says that "[we] lead by word and deed *simply because [we are] here doing what [we] do.*" In what ways do you exercise leadership wherever you might be by simply doing what you do?

Prayers of Hope & Healing

Pray that we all might have the wisdom to know when to step up and lead and when to step back and follow.

Prayer for Today

Guiding God, "teach me the way I should go," and I will know better how to lead and how to follow. Amen.

Notes

Day 25

CAN WE HELP EACH OTHER deal with the inner issues inherent in leadership? We can, and I believe we must. . . . First, we could lift up the value of "inner work." That phrase should become commonplace in families, schools, and religious institutions, at least, helping us understand that inner work is as real as outer work and involves skills one can develop, skills like journaling, reflective reading, spiritual friendship, meditation, and prayer. We can teach our children something that their parents did not always know: if people skimp on their inner work, their outer work will suffer as well.

Second, we could spread the word that inner work, though it is a deeply *personal* matter, is not necessarily a *private* matter: inner work can be helped along in community. Indeed, doing inner work together is a vital counterpoint to doing it alone. Left to our own devices, we may delude ourselves in ways that others help us correct.

⌒

BIBLICAL WISDOM

I pray that, according to the riches of his glory, he may grant that you may be strengthened in your inner being with power through his Spirit. . . .
Ephesians 3:16

SILENCE FOR MEDITATION

QUESTIONS TO PONDER

- In our culture, to what degree do you think that families, schools, and religious institutions value inner work? Why?
- What is the evidence that if people skimp on their inner work, their outer work will suffer as well?
- Palmer states that "inner work can be helped along in community." Is that true in your faith community? Why or why not?

PSALM FRAGMENT

I commune with my heart in the night;
  I meditate and search my spirit. Psalm 77:6

JOURNAL REFLECTIONS

- Palmer states that inner work involves "skills one can develop, skills like journaling, reflective reading, spiritual friendship, meditation, and prayer." Write about the place of these practices in your life. Which are you presently doing? Which would you like to develop? What resources are available to help you grow in these practices?
- Reflect on whether you are—or are not—comfortable doing inner work together with someone else.
- As Palmer notes, inner work is very personal. To what degree are you open to feedback from others with respect to your inner work?

PRAYERS OF HOPE & HEALING

Pray that we would all find both secular and sacred communities that encourage and support us in our inner work.

PRAYER FOR TODAY

Holy One, may I be disciplined today in balancing my outer work with inner work. Amen.

NOTES

Day 26

SEASONS IS A WISE METAPHOR for the movement of life. . . . The notion that our lives are like the eternal cycle of the seasons does not deny the struggle or the joy, the loss or the gain, the darkness or the light, but encourages us to embrace it all—and to find in all of it opportunities for growth.

If we lived close to nature in an agricultural society, the seasons as metaphor and fact would continually frame our lives. But the master metaphor of our era does not come from agriculture—it comes from manufacturing. We do not believe that we "grow" our lives—we believe that we "make" them. Just listen to how we use the word in everyday speech: we make time, make friends, make meaning, make money, make a living, make love.

I once heard Alan Watts observe that a Chinese child will ask, "How does a baby grow?" But an American child will ask, "How do you make a baby?" From an early age we absorb our culture's arrogant conviction that we manufacture everything, reducing the world to mere "raw material" that lacks all value until we impose our designs and labor on it.

If we accept the notion that our lives are dependent on an inexorable cycle of seasons, on a play of powers that we can conspire with but never control, we run headlong into a culture that insists, against all evidence, that we can make whatever kind of life we want, whenever we want it. Deeper still we run headlong into our own egos, which want desperately to believe that we are always in charge.

BIBLICAL WISDOM

For everything there is a season, and a time for every matter under heaven.
Ecclesiastes 3:1

SILENCE FOR MEDITATION

Questions to Ponder

- As a metaphor for life, what rings more true for you: the organic metaphor of growth or the mechanistic metaphor of manufacturing?
- What are the attitudes and behaviors that flow from believing that we "make" our lives?
- What are the attitudes and behaviors that flow from believing that we "grow" our lives?

Psalm Fragment

The eyes of all look to you,
and you give them their food in due season.
You open your hand,
satisfying the desire of every living thing. Psalm 145:15-16

Journal Reflections

- Meditate on the different feelings, attitudes, and behaviors that are evoked by changing "we make time, make friends, make meaning, make money, make a living, make love" to "we grow time, grow friends, grow meaning, grow money, grow a living, grow love."
- Does it comfort or frighten you to know that "our lives are dependent on an inexorable cycle of seasons, on a play of powers that we can conspire with but never control"? Explain.
- With respect to the deeper movements of life, how comfortable are you with the fact that you are not in charge?

Prayers of Hope & Healing

Pray for the "movers and shakers," that they might slow down enough to smell the roses and then get caught up in wonder at the mystery of roses.

Prayer for Today

God of life and death, may I have the wisdom to go with the flow of the seasons of my life. Amen.

Notes

AUTUMN IS A SEASON OF great beauty, but it is also a season of decline: the days grow shorter, the light is suffused, and summer's abundance decays towards winter's death. Faced with this inevitable winter, what does nature do in autumn? It scatters the seeds that will bring new growth in the spring—and scatters them with amazing abandon. . . . As I explore autumn's paradox of dying and seeding, I feel the power of metaphor. In the autumnal events of my own experience, I am easily fixated on the decline of meaning, the decay of relationships, the death of a work. And yet if I look more deeply, I may see the myriad possibilities being planted to bear fruit in some season yet to come. . . .

This hopeful notion that living is hidden within dying is surely enhanced by the visual glories of autumn. What artist would ever have painted a season of dying with such a vivid palette if nature had not done it first. Does death possess a beauty that we—who fear death, who find it ugly and obscene—cannot see? How shall we understand autumn's testimony that death and elegance go hand in hand?

For me, the words that come closest to answering those questions are the words of Thomas Merton: "There is in all visible things . . . a hidden wholeness."[11] In the visible world of nature, a great truth is concealed in plain sight: diminishment and beauty, darkness and light, death and life are not opposites. They are held together in the paradox of "hidden wholeness."

BIBLICAL WISDOM

Ever since the creation of the world his eternal power and divine nature, invisible though they are, have been understood and seen through the things he has made.
Romans 1:20

SILENCE FOR MEDITATION

Questions to Ponder

- In what ways is it evident that our culture lives in denial of death?
- In what way is autumn's paradox of dying and seeding a hopeful reality?
- "How shall we understand autumn's testimony that death and elegance go hand in hand?"

Psalm Fragment

Lord, let me know my end,
and what is the measure of my days;
let me know how fleeting my life is. Psalm 39:4

Journal Reflections

- What are the autumnal events of your own experience?
- In these autumnal events, have you been able to discover the myriad possibilities being planted to bear fruit in some season yet to come? Explain.
- Meditate on death and write your thoughts and feelings.

Prayers of Hope & Healing

Pray for those who are suffering loss and disappointment, that "autumn's paradox of dying and seeding" might give them hope.

Prayer for Today

God of all comfort, open my eyes to see death as you see death. Amen.

Notes

Day 28

OUR INWARD WINTERS TAKE MANY forms—failure, betrayal, depression, death. But every one of them, in my experience, yields to the same advice: "The winters will drive you crazy unless you learn to get out into them." Until we enter boldly into the fears we want to avoid, those fears will dominate our lives. But when we walk directly into them—protected from frostbite by the warm garb of friendship or inner discipline or spiritual guidance—we can learn what they have to teach us. Then we discover once again that the cycle of the seasons is trustworthy and life-giving, even in the most dismaying season of all.

BIBLICAL WISDOM

Some friends play at friendship
but a true friend sticks closer than one's nearest kin. Proverbs 18:24

SILENCE FOR MEDITATION

QUESTIONS TO PONDER

- Explain how the saying that "the winters will drive you crazy unless you learn to get out into them" applies to our inward winters.
- Do you agree that our inward winters have something to teach us? Why or why not?
- What would be the results of resisting or denying instead of entering our inward winters?

PSALM FRAGMENT

Even though I walk through the darkest valley,
I fear no evil;
for you are with me;
your rod and your staff—
they comfort me. Psalm 23:4

JOURNAL REFLECTIONS

- Palmer states that "our inward winters take many forms—failure, betrayal, depression, death." Describe some of the inward winters you have experienced.
- What (and who) helped you to get out into and live through your inward winters?
- Through the experience, did you discover that "the cycle of the seasons is trustworthy and life-giving, even in the most dismaying season of all"? Explain.

PRAYERS OF HOPE & HEALING

Pray that those who find themselves in the darkest winter would be "protected from frostbite by the warm garb of friendship or inner discipline or spiritual guidance."

PRAYER FOR TODAY

God of nature, in the cold of winter let me trust the coming warmth of spring. Amen.

NOTES

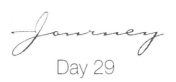

BEFORE SPRING BECOMES BEAUTIFUL, IT is plug ugly, nothing but mud and muck. I have walked in the early spring through fields that will suck your boots off, a world so wet and woeful it makes you yearn for the return of ice. But in that muddy mess, the conditions for rebirth are being created.

I love the fact that the word *humus*—the decayed vegetable matter that feeds the roots of plants—comes from the same root that gives rise to the word *humility*. It is a blessed etymology. It helps me understand that the humiliating events of life, the events that leave "mud on my face" or that "make my name mud," may create the fertile soil in which something new can grow. . . .

In my own life, as my winters segue into spring, I find it not only hard to cope with mud but also hard to credit the small harbingers of larger life to come, hard to hope until the outcome is secure. Spring teaches me to look more carefully for the green stems of possibility: for the intuitive hunch that may turn into a larger insight, for the glance or touch that may thaw a frozen relationship, for the stranger's act of kindness that makes the world seem hospitable again.

BIBLICAL WISDOM

Blessed are those who mourn, for they will be comforted.
Blessed are the meek, for they will inherit the earth. Matthew 5:4-5

SILENCE FOR MEDITATION

QUESTIONS TO PONDER

- Is the fact that "before spring becomes beautiful, it is plug ugly, nothing but mud and muck" a good metaphor for you in the light of your own experience with inward winters? Explain.
- How do you understand the word *humility*?

- How might the humiliating events of life actually bring creative possibilities?

PSALM FRAGMENT

He leads the humble in what is right,
and teaches the humble his way. Psalm 25:9

JOURNAL REFLECTIONS

- Write about some of the humiliating events in your life that have led to positive growth for you.
- As your inward winters segued into spring, how did you cope with the mud?
- Read the last paragraph of today's reading again. What has spring taught you to look more carefully for?

PRAYERS OF HOPE & HEALING

Pray for those whose feet are stuck in the muck of early spring, that they might be encouraged and sustained by the promise of burgeoning life in late spring.

PRAYER FOR TODAY

God of the seasons, thank you for the promise of spring that can come at any time. Amen.

NOTES

Day 30

WHERE I LIVE, SUMMER'S KEYNOTE is abundance. . . . This fact of nature is in sharp contrast to human nature, which seems to regard perpetual scarcity as the law of life. Daily I am astonished at how readily I believe that something that I need is in short supply. If I hoard possessions, it is because I believe that there are not enough to go around. If I struggle with others over power, it is because I believe that power is limited. If I become jealous in relationships, it is because I believe that when you get too much love I will be short-changed. . . .

Authentic abundance does not lie in secured stockpiles of food or cash or influence of affection but in belonging to a community where we can give those goods to others who need them—and receive them from others when we are in need. . . .

Here is a summertime truth: abundance is a communal act, the joint creation of an incredibly complex ecology in which each part functions on behalf of the whole and, in return, is sustained by the whole. Community doesn't just create abundance—community *is* abundance. If we could learn that equation from the world of nature, the human world might be transformed.

⌁

BIBLICAL WISDOM

I do not mean that there should be relief for others and pressure on you, but it is a question of a fair balance between your present abundance and their need, so that their abundance may be for your need, in order that there may be a fair balance. As it is written,
  "The one who had much did not have too much,
  and the one who had little did not have too little." 2 Corinthians 8:13-15

SILENCE FOR MEDITATION

QUESTIONS TO PONDER

• Today's reading implies that abundance does not mean *having a lot.* What does it mean?

- Palmer states that "community doesn't just create abundance—community *is* abundance." Do you agree? Why or why not?
- Read today's *Biblical Wisdom* again. Is the vision of secular and sacred communities—where the one who had much did not have too much and the one who had little did not have too little—realistic, hopelessly idealistic, or somewhere in between? Explain.

PSALM FRAGMENT

May there be abundance of grain in the land;
  may it wave on the tops of the mountains;
  may its fruit be like Lebanon;
  and may people blossom in the cities
  like the grass of the field. Psalm 72:16

JOURNAL REFLECTIONS

- Palmer admits that "daily I am astonished at how readily I believe that something that I need is in short supply." Does that ring true for you as well? Why or why not?
- Meditate on the give and take of community as Palmer describes it. Have you experienced such community? If so, describe the experience. If not, what do you imagine it would be like?
- Write about the risks you might face in helping to transform a secular or sacred community into a place where everyone functions on behalf of the whole and, in return, is sustained by the whole.

PRAYERS OF HOPE & HEALING

Pray for the sacred and secular communities of which you are a part, that they might be places where the abundance that God gives and intends for all is shared by all.

PRAYER FOR TODAY

Sustaining God, let me be content and confident today, trusting in the "summertime truth" that there is enough for all of us to thrive if all of us share. Amen.

NOTES

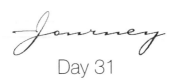

Day 31

THE ACTIVE LIFE TAKES MANY forms, [among them] work, creativity, and caring. . . . Work is action driven by external necessity or demand. We work because we need to make a living, because we need to solve a problem, because we need to surmount or survive. I do not mean that we are mere robots when we work, totally determined by factors outside ourselves; we may choose whether to work, when to work, how to work. But work, as I use the word here, always involves the element of necessity, and that element leads to the characteristic dilemmas of this form of the active life.

Creativity, in contrast, is driven more by inner choice than by outer demand. An act cannot be creative if it is not born of freedom. In creative action, our desire is not to "solve" or "succeed" or "survive" but to give birth to something new; we want, for a while, to be less creaturely and more like the creator. If work reveals something of our bondage to the world, creativity reveals something of how we transcend it—and that fact gives rise to the dilemmas of creativity.

Caring is also action freely chosen. But in caring we aim not at giving birth to something new; we aim at nurturing, protecting, guiding, healing, or empowering something that already has life. The energy behind caring is compassion for others which, in turn, is energized by the knowledge that we are all in this together, that the fate of other human beings has implications for our own fate. Caring may take a personal form, for instance, when we comfort a grieving friend. But it can also take form through movements for political and economic justice, in speaking on behalf of strangers whose oppression diminishes us all.

᷎

BIBLICAL WISDOM

But we were gentle among you, like a nurse tenderly caring for her own children. So deeply do we care for you that we are determined to share with you not only the gospel of God but also our own selves, because you have become very dear to us.
1 Thessalonians 2:7b-8

SILENCE FOR MEDITATION

QUESTIONS TO PONDER

- What are the dilemmas that result from the fact that work always involves the element of necessity?
- Our culture has a tendency to reduce both creativity and the artifacts of creativity to commodities. What affect does this have on the creative spirit? How can this tendency be resisted?
- Palmer stresses that the "knowledge that we are all in this together" energizes compassion for others, which leads to acts of caring. Why do so many of us seem to resist that knowledge?

PSALM FRAGMENT

People go out to their work
and to their labor until the evening. Psalm 104:23

JOURNAL REFLECTIONS

- Write about your work—both paid work and unpaid work. Explore the level of satisfaction and meaning that comes from your work. To what degree does your work express your inner truth?
- Write about your creative pursuits. What are you trying to give birth to, or reveal, or express? How does your choice to be creative give meaning, purpose, and joy to other areas of your life?
- Write about the ways in which caring, compassion, and a passion for the good of others are expressed in your personal and public life. How does your caring express itself in your work and creative pursuits?

PRAYERS OF HOPE & HEALING

Pray that we all might experience that convergence of work, creativity, and caring that brings richness and joy to everyday life.

PRAYER FOR TODAY

Creator God, remind me throughout the day that I am your cocreator in fashioning a world of love and justice. Amen.

NOTES

Journey
Day 32

THE FUNCTION OF CONTEMPLATION IN all its forms is to penetrate illusion and help us to touch reality. Contemplation is difficult for many of us because we have invested so much in illusion. Sometimes we even seem wedded to illusion as a way of survival. When I look at my own life I am appalled at the illusions I have cultivated simply to get me through the day—illusions about my motives, my abilities, my desires. I am appalled at the pain that my illusions have caused me and others, and at the thought that right now I harbor illusions I cannot even name because I depend on the belief that they are real.

When I look at the society around me, I see illusions as thick as my own: the illusion that violence solves problems, that both rich and poor deserve their fate, that young people sent to die in wars fought to defend the rich are heroes rather than victims, that murderous drugs are the way beyond despair—just to name a few.

BIBLICAL WISDOM

For they are a rebellious people,
faithless children,
children who will not hear
the instruction of the LORD;
who say to the seers, "Do not see";
and to the prophets, "Do not prophesy to us what is right;
speak to us smooth things,
prophesy illusions." Isaiah 30:9-10

SILENCE FOR MEDITATION

QUESTIONS TO PONDER

- Parker states that "the function of contemplation in all its forms is to penetrate illusion and help us to touch reality." What are the various forms of contemplation and how do they help us to penetrate illusion?

- If you believe an illusion, it seems true and not an illusion at all. How can we resist our tendency to deceive ourselves? What role might other people have in helping us to unmask our illusions?
- Society and culture perpetuate illusions. Reread the last paragraph of today's reading. Reflect on how these social illusions control our attitudes and behaviors. What other social illusions might you add to Palmer's list?

PSALM FRAGMENT

Put false ways far from me;
and graciously teach me your law. Psalm 119:29

JOURNAL REFLECTIONS

- Palmer admits to illusions about his motives, his abilities, and his desires, illusions he has come to be aware of. Write about illusions regarding your own motives, abilities, and desires that you have become aware of. How does this awareness feel?
- Palmer also admits that he is appalled "at the thought that right now I harbor illusions I cannot even name because I depend on the belief that they are real." How can one begin to expose such "thick" illusions? How can others help us?
- What role should your community of faith play in helping to unmask social/cultural illusions?

PRAYERS OF HOPE & HEALING

Pray that we all might more clearly see the "pain" our illusions cause ourselves and others so we might begin to put "false ways" far from us.

PRAYER FOR TODAY

God of truth, even if it is painful, open my eyes that I might see what is real and what is not real. Amen.

NOTES

Journey

Day 33

THERE IS THE EXPERIENCE WE commonly call *disillusionment,* when a trusted friend lets us down, an institution we had relied on fails us, a vision we had believed in turns out to be a hoax, or—worst of all—when we discover ourselves to be less than we had thought. Many of us try hard to avoid such experiences, and when we are in the midst of them we go through a kind of dying. But the very name we give these moments tells us that something positive is happening through our pain. We say we are being "dis-illusioned." That is, we are being stripped of some illusions about life, about others, about ourselves. As our illusions are removed, like barriers on a road, we have a chance to take that road farther toward truth. Instead of commiserating and offering a shoulder to cry on when a friend says that he or she is disillusioned, we ought to congratulate, celebrate, and ask the friend how we can help the process go deeper still.

⌒

BIBLICAL WISDOM

For whoever finds [Wisdom] finds life
and obtains favor from the LORD;
but those who miss me injure themselves;
all who hate me love death. Proverbs 8:35-36

SILENCE FOR MEDITATION

QUESTIONS TO PONDER

- How does it feel to think about the experience of disillusionment as something to be embraced rather than avoided at all costs?
- How do our experiences of disillusionment change when we see them as learning experiences or opportunities to be "dis-illusioned"?
- Have you ever been congratulated on being disillusioned? If so, what was it like? If not, can you imagine such an experience?

PSALM FRAGMENT

You desire truth in the inward being;
therefore teach me wisdom in my secret heart. Psalm 51:6

JOURNAL REFLECTIONS

- Write about a time when you were disillusioned about yourself, some-one else, or some institution. What was it like? Was it a positive learning experience? Were you able to shed any illusions? How did it affect your life moving forward?
- With a friend who is disillusioned, is your first inclination to commiserate with him or her or to invite the friend to celebrate? Explain. After today will you respond differently?
- Disillusionment is a beginning stage of growth. How can we help the process go deeper still?

PRAYERS OF HOPE & HEALING

Pray that we would all be able to celebrate without sarcasm or judgment or condescension when our friends are dis-illusioned.

PRAYER FOR TODAY

Holy One, let there be people in my life who can celebrate my learning experiences even when they are painful. Amen.

NOTES

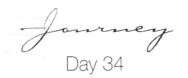

Day 34

SOLITUDE IS NOT SIMPLY PHYSICAL isolation. It is easy to be alone and yet continue to be in the crowd, to be governed by collective values, and it is possible to be physically in the midst of a crowd and yet to be in solitude. To be in solitude means to be in possession of my own heart, my identity, my integrity. It means to refuse to let my life and my meanings be dictated by other people or by an impersonal culture. To be in solitude is to claim my birthright of aliveness on its own terms, terms that respect the life around me but do not demean my own. The solitary is someone who, to paraphrase Merton, is able to give her heart away because it is in her possession to give—a possession not possible when we are caught in the silent conspiracy of collective illusions.

BIBLICAL WISDOM

And after he had dismissed the crowds, he went up the mountain by himself to pray. When evening came, he was there alone. Matthew 14:23

SILENCE FOR MEDITATION

QUESTIONS TO PONDER

- Give examples of how one might "be alone and yet continue to be in the crowd, to be governed by collective values."
- The evidence—the constant use of cell phones, instant messaging, e-mail, chat rooms, MP3 players, and so forth—suggests that North Americans flee solitude. Why do you think this is so?
- What do you think it means to be in possession of your own heart?

PSALM FRAGMENT

Be still before the LORD, and wait patiently for him. Psalm 37:7a

Journal Reflections

- Reflect on the way you live. What are the ways in which you embrace solitude? What are the ways in which you flee solitude?
- In what ways do you feel in possession of your own heart, identity, integrity?
- In what ways do you feel that your life and meanings are dictated by other people or an impersonal culture?

Prayers of Hope & Healing

Pray that we all might experience the wonder of possessing our own hearts enough that we are free to give them away.

Prayer for Today

God, you who speak with a still small voice, let me love my own solitude and respect the solitude of others. Amen.

Notes

Day 35

IF WE WANT TO BREAK out of the mechanistic and obsessive sort of action . . . we must first learn to ask ourselves a simple question: "Why am I doing this?" This is the question of motives, and we hardly ever ask it of ourselves (though we are sometimes quick to inspect, and suspect, the motives of other people). Every action has some motive behind it, some impetus, a force-field out of which it arises. If we do not explore that force we will never act in a transcendent way; we will live out our active lives as automatons who move but do not choose. . . .

Many of us act from motives that are not entirely benign, on terms that are not always our own. We may act, not by choice, but on demand; not for ourselves and our own reasons, but for others and their reasons; not for the sake of the act itself, but for the sake of the money or security or approval or prestige it will bring; not because we love working, but because we want to avoid the guilt of not working. Motives such as these are so common that we accept them as the inevitable launching pads of action.

But a launching pad is only temporary; once launched, the rocket is free of the pad's constraints. We often must launch our actions from motives and circumstances that are less than ideal. If we wait for the ideal motives before we act, most of us would never act; but if we allow our action to be confined by its original motives, our action may be slipshod, graceless, banal. What is the process by which we . . . might accept an undesirable impetus to action and yet allow our action to be transformed into something of beauty and truth that transcends its original constraints?

BIBLICAL WISDOM

Do not be conformed to this world, but be transformed by the renewing of your minds, so that you may discern what is the will of God—what is good and acceptable and perfect. Romans 12:2

SILENCE FOR MEDITATION

Questions to Ponder

- Why do you think so many people in our society resist questioning their motives and don't ask that simple question: "Why am I doing this?"
- Palmer notes that "many of us act from motives that are not entirely benign, on terms that are not always our own." How can such action be transformed into something of beauty and truth?
- Faith communities also act from motives and also often resist questioning their motives. How can a faith community be more self-critical about its motives?

Psalm Fragment

Search me, O God, and know my heart;
  test me and know my thoughts.
See if there is any wicked way in me,
  and lead me in the way everlasting. Psalm 139:23-24

Journal Reflections

- Make a list of the things you do—work-related, volunteer-related, relationship-related—and then after each entry in your list write the answer to the question: Why am I doing this?
- What conclusions can you draw about your motives from this exercise?
- If some of your motives are not entirely benign, in what ways might your action be transformed into something of beauty and truth?

Prayers of Hope & Healing

Pray that we would all have clarity as to why we do what we do, and that our motives would match our values, and our values would be expressed in our action.

Prayer for Today

God of light, today I will not live by default, but will consciously make the choices that move me to act. Amen.

Notes

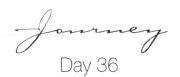
Day 36

EVERY HUMAN BEING IS BORN with some sort of gift, an inclination or instinct that can become a full-blown mastery. We may not see our gift for what it is. Having seen it, we may choose not to accept the gift and its consequences for our lives. Or, having claimed our gift, we may not be willing to do the hard work necessary to nurture it. But none of these evasions can alter the fact that the gift is ours. Each of us is a master at something, and part of becoming fully alive is to discover and develop our birthright competence.

Discerning our native gifts is difficult for many reasons. We live in a culture that tells us there is no such thing as a gift, that we must earn or make everything we get. Social forces such as racism, sexism, and ageism press poor self-images upon us. Various inner pathologies may lead us to embrace those images despite the obvious damage they do. But the most subtle barrier to the discernment of our native gifts is in the gifts themselves: they are so central to us, so integral to who we are, that we take them for granted and are often utterly unaware of the mastery they give us.

BIBLICAL WISDOM

But each has a particular gift from God, one having one kind and another a different kind. 1 Corinthians 7:7b

SILENCE FOR MEDITATION

QUESTIONS TO PONDER

- How do you account for the fact that so many people don't seem to believe they have a gift that can become a full-blown mastery?
- Is it ever too late to discover, claim, and begin developing your gift? Explain.
- There are many social forces that work against our discovering, claiming, and developing our gift. How might a faith community help to overcome the influence of those social forces?

PSALM FRAGMENT

Praise him with trumpet sound;
  praise him with lute and harp!
Praise him with tambourine and dance;
  praise him with strings and pipe!
Praise him with clanging cymbals;
  praise him with loud clashing cymbals!
Let everything that breathes praise the LORD!
Praise the LORD! Psalm 150:3-6

JOURNAL REFLECTIONS

- What does it feel like to read that you are "born with some sort of a gift . . . that can become a full-blown mastery"?
- Are you aware of what your gift is? If so, describe it. If not, wait for tomorrow's reading and journaling exercises.
- Do you feel any pressures (from other people or from society) to resist the idea that you are a master at something? Explain.

PRAYERS OF HOPE & HEALING

Pray that those who believe they have no gift would discover their gift, claim their gift, and begin to nurture their gift.

PRAYER FOR TODAY

Holy One, let me walk along the road toward mastery today. Amen.

NOTES

Day 37

So when we seek our own birthright gifts, it is important not to equate them with the techniques our society names as skills. Our gifts may be as simple as a real interest in other people, a quiet and caring manner, an eye for beauty, a love of rhythm and sound. But in those simple, personal gifts, the seeds of vocation are often found, if we are willing to do the inner and outer work necessary to cultivate our mastery.

Some readers may remain unconvinced that everyone is born with some gift, some mastery. For them—wounded perhaps by an ego or a culture that says people are incompetent without training—the notion that we are all given expertise at birth may sound like the largest illusion of all. I cannot offer definite proof of this claim for people who do not intuit its truth, but I can offer some supportive evidence.

Over the past decade a new approach to vocation seeking has emerged that draws on the insights of *depth psychology*. In this approach people are encouraged to begin, not with their credentials, but with the question, "What are my leading gifts and abilities?" There are various ways to answer this question, but many of the new career counselors urge people to start by writing a childhood autobiography. Some job-seekers find it odd to explore their earliest childhood memories of how they spent time, what brought them pleasure, what they could not abide. . . . Some of the most powerful clues to our true gifts are buried deep in childhood, when we said and did and felt things without censoring them through external values or expectations.

~

BIBLICAL WISDOM

Ask, and it will be given you; search, and you will find; knock, and the door will be opened for you. For everyone who asks receives, and everyone who searches finds, and for everyone who knocks, the door will be opened. Matthew 7:7-8

SILENCE FOR MEDITATION

QUESTIONS TO PONDER

- Are you (or are you not) convinced that everyone is born with some gift, some mastery? Explain.
- What differences would there be between birthright gifts and skills? What relationship might there be between gifts and skills?
- What would be more important in choosing a vocation, birthright gifts or learned techniques or skills? Explain.

PSALM FRAGMENT

God, our God, has blessed us.
May God continue to bless us;
*   let all the ends of the earth revere him.* Psalm 67:6b-7

JOURNAL REFLECTIONS

- In your journal write a childhood autobiography. How did you spend your time? What brought you pleasure? What kind of people did you like to be with? What kind of people did you avoid? What could you not abide with?
- Read through your autobiography again. Do you find any clues to your true gifts and abilities? Are they gifts you have been aware of or gifts you are just becoming aware of? Explain.
- If you found clues to your true gifts in writing your childhood autobiography, how might you begin (or continue) to claim and cultivate them?

PRAYERS OF HOPE & HEALING

Pray for those who spend their time doing things they *have been trained to do* but find no satisfaction in, that they might recover the joys of their childhood.

PRAYER FOR TODAY

Loving God, today let me have a childlike joy in what I do and who I am. Amen.

NOTES

Journey

Day 38

EVERY LIFE IS LIVED TOWARD a horizon, a distant vision of what lies ahead. The quality of our action depends heavily on whether that horizon is dark with death or full of light and life. When we imagine ourselves moving toward the finality of death, our action may become deformed. We may become paralyzed, unable to act freely. We may become driven by fear, obsessed with protecting and preserving what we have, which is a sure way of losing it. With death on our horizon we may act in ways aimed at getting it over with, ways that lead to self-destruction now simply because destruction seems inevitable. But when we envision a horizon which holds the hope of life, we are free to act without fear, free to act in truth and love and justice today because those very qualities seem to shape our own destiny.

BIBLICAL WISDOM

Then I saw a new heaven and a new earth; for the first heaven and the first earth had passed away. . . . And I heard a loud voice from the throne saying,
"See, the home of God is among mortals.
He will dwell with them as their God;
they will be his peoples,
and God himself will be with them;
he will wipe every tear from their eyes.
Death will be no more;
mourning and crying and pain will be no more,
for the first things have passed away." Revelation 21:1-4

SILENCE FOR MEDITATION

QUESTIONS TO PONDER

• What evidence do you find that for much of our culture the horizon is dark with death?

- How does this apparent movement toward the finality of death affect the quality of action in our culture?
- Where do you find signs in our culture that there are those who envision a horizon that holds the hope of life? How does that vision affect the quality of their action?

PSALM FRAGMENT

For you have delivered my soul from death,
    and my feet from falling,
    so that I may walk before God
    in the light of life. Psalm 56:13

JOURNAL REFLECTIONS

- What horizon, what distant vision of what lies ahead, are you living toward?
- Write in a stream of consciousness fashion about your attitude toward death.
- How does your understanding of what ultimately lies ahead shape your decisions, your relationships, and your action in the world?

PRAYERS OF HOPE & HEALING

Pray for those whose horizon is cramped and dark, that they would be graced with a vision of life endlessly opening up before them.

PRAYER FOR TODAY

God of life, even though I walk through the valley of the shadow of death,
    I fear no evil; for you are with me. Amen.

NOTES

Day 39

IF WE HAVE A SIDE that is fearful of life and attracted to death, it would help to explain why our world seems so dominated by death and its agents. Why do we go so easily to war, even in an age when doomsday weapons could destroy all life? Why are we so drawn to "entertainment" that involves depictions of violence and killing? Why do we so readily embrace the notion that there are "acceptable levels of death" from carcinogenic chemicals and nuclear power plants? Perhaps because we are afraid of life, of its challenges and demands for change. Perhaps because we perversely prefer the safe and predictable confines of the grave.

~

BIBLICAL WISDOM

In the path of righteousness there is life,
  in walking its path there is no death. Proverbs 12:28

SILENCE FOR MEDITATION

QUESTIONS TO PONDER

- Why would anyone be fearful of life?
- How do you account for the fact that so many of the world's great religions, which ostensibly revere life, so often participate in their culture's choosing of death?
- What does it take to choose life in a world that so often chooses violence and death?

PSALM FRAGMENT

For you have delivered my soul from death,
  my eyes from tears,
  my feet from stumbling.
I walk before the LORD
  in the land of the living. Psalm 116:8-9

JOURNAL REFLECTIONS

- Would you say that you are afraid or unafraid (or somewhere in between) of life's challenges and demands for change?
- What resources do you have for facing life's challenges and demands for change?
- In what ways do your actions and attitudes reflect a reverence for all life?

PRAYERS OF HOPE & HEALING

Pray for those who accept in resignation or are indifferent to whatever diminishes, damages, or destroys life, that they might learn to say no to such things.

PRAYER FOR TODAY

God of all blessing, let my life be a blessing. Amen.

NOTES

Journey

Day 40

SINCE DEATH IS OUR CONSTANT companion whether we like it or not, it must be "marvelous" to live in a dialogue with death in which life gets the final word. . . .

It is a simple fact that we live while dying, that every minute of life brings us closer to death. But our encounter with that fact is painful at first, and there is much in us that wants to evade the pain by denying death as long as we can.

When we live in illusion, denying reality, resisting the inevitable, we live in a tension that drains us of energy without our even knowing it. So if we try to gain life by denying death, the paradoxical result is that we become lifeless. This is why "dis-illusionment" is so important, for by losing our illusions we can tap the energy of the reality that lies beyond them. Once we are thoroughly dis-illusioned we can say with Thoreau, "Reality is fabulous!" No matter how difficult reality may be, it contains more life than any illusion.

BIBLICAL WISDOM

Who will separate us from the love of Christ? Will hardship, or distress, or persecution, or famine, or nakedness, or peril, or sword?. . . No, in all these things we are more than conquerors through him who loved us. For I am convinced that neither death, nor life, nor angels, nor rulers, nor things present, nor things to come, nor powers, nor height, nor depth, nor anything else in all creation, will be able to separate us from the love of God in Christ Jesus our Lord. Romans 8:35, 37-39

SILENCE FOR MEDITATION

QUESTIONS TO PONDER

- What does it mean to say that life gets the final word?
- What would a person's life look like if he or she lived in a dialogue with death in which life gets the final word?

- What would a secular or sacred community look like if it engaged in a dialogue with death in which life gets the final word?

PSALM FRAGMENT

The LORD is gracious and merciful,
slow to anger and abounding in steadfast love.
The LORD is good to all,
and his compassion is over all that he has made. Psalm 145:8-9

JOURNAL REFLECTIONS

- How comfortable are you with the "simple fact that we live while dying"? Explain.
- As a result of this 40-day journey with Parker J. Palmer, are you more inclined or less inclined to agree with Thoreau's claim that "Reality is fabulous!" Explain.
- Having completed this 40-day journey, how would you answer these two questions now: Who am I meant to be? What am I meant to do?

PRAYERS OF HOPE & HEALING

Pray for all who continue in their quest for wholeness, that their feet would stay on the path and they would know joy.

PRAYER FOR TODAY

God of all wisdom, you who are "a lamp to my feet and a light to my path," thank you for this 40-day journey. Amen.

NOTES

JOURNEY'S END

You have finished your *40-Day Journey with Parker J. Palmer*. I hope it has been a good journey and that along the way you have learned much, experienced much, and found good resources to deepen your faith and practice. As a result of this journey:

- How are you different?
- What have you learned?
- What have you experienced?
- In what ways has your faith and practice been transformed?

NOTES

Do you want to continue the journey? If you would, there is a list of books by Parker J. Palmer on the next page that will help you delve further into the thought, experience, and practice of this remarkable spiritual teacher and guide.

FOR FURTHER READING

The Courage to Teach: Exploring the Inner Landscape of a Teacher's Life. San Francisco: Jossey-Bass, 2007.

A Hidden Wholeness: The Journey Toward an Undivided Life. San Francisco: Jossey-Bass, 2004.

Let Your Life Speak: Listening for the Voice of Vocation. San Francisco: Jossey-Bass, 2000.

To Know as We Are Known: Education as a Spiritual Journey. New York: HarperOne, 1993.

The Active Life: A Spirituality of Work, Creativity, and Caring. San Francisco: Jossey-Bass, 1990.

The Company of Strangers: Christians & the Renewal of America's Public Life. New York: Crossroad 1983.

The Promise of Paradox. Notre Dame, Ind.: Ave Maria, 1980. (The readings from *The Promise of Paradox* in this book were taken from the 1980 edition. A new edition of *The Promise of Paradox* was published in April 2008 by Jossey-Bass, San Francisco.)

SOURCES

ENDNOTES

1 Henri J. M. Nouwen, "Introduction," in Parker J. Palmer, *The Promise of Paradox* (Notre Dame, Ind.: Ave Maria, 1980), 11–12.
2 The title of a 2004 book by Parker J. Palmer (see For Further Reading above).
3 Parker J. Palmer, *The Active Life* (San Francisco: Jossey-Bass, 1999), 155.
4 Parker J. Palmer, *Let Your Life Speak* (San Francisco: Jossey-Bass, 2000), 19.
5 In *Let Your Life Speak,* the author uses his own journey toward inner integrity and vocation as a map guiding others on the journey. It is the book to read if you are interested in Parker J. Palmer's spiritual and psychological journey toward wholeness.
6 Palmer, *Let Your Life Speak,* 52, 53.
7 Mary Oliver, "Maybe," in *The Soul Is Hear for Its Own Joy: Sacred Poems from Many Cultures,* ed. Robert Bly (Hopewell, N.J.: Ecco, 1995), 4.
8 Dietrich Bonhoeffer, *Life Together* (New York: HarperCollins, 1954), 78.
9 William Stafford, "Ask Me," in *The Way It Is: New & Selected Poems* (St. Paul: Graywolf, 1998), 56.
10 Ibid.
11 Thomas Merton, "Hagia Sophia," in *A Thomas Merton Reader,* ed. Thomas P. McDonnell (New York: Harper's Magazine Press, 1974), 129–30.

NOTES

NOTES

NOTES

Made in the USA
Lexington, KY
07 November 2012